Juicing For Beginners

Simple Juice Cookbook With Recipes for Health, Weight Loss, Vitality Boost, Anti-Aging, Detox And Longevity.

Includes a 30-Day Meal Plan

KARA KEMP

Kara Kemp

TABLE OF CONTENTS

Juicing for beginners

Kara Kemp

Introduction

Welcome to the vibrant and health-boosting world of juicing. Whether you're seeking a new tool to enhance your health, find a fun way to consume your fruits and vegetables or explore the vast landscape of natural flavors, this guide, "Juicing for Beginners," is here to embark on this journey with you.

Juicing has gained popularity over the years due to its convenience, nutrient-packed offerings, and the simplicity of integrating it into our daily routines. What began as a niche trend among health enthusiasts has become mainstream, making it a staple in homes worldwide.

Before we dive into the intricacies of juicing, let's clarify what it is exactly. Juicing is extracting the liquid from fruits and vegetables, leaving the pulp behind. The resulting liquid is a nutritionally dense "juice" containing most vitamins, minerals, and phytochemicals in the fruit or vegetable.

This guide will serve as your compass, navigating you through the basics of juicing and beyond. We will delve into the types of juicers available and how to choose the one best suited to your needs. We will explore the vast array of fruits and vegetables that can be juiced, their health benefits, and how to prepare them for juicing. You'll find many beginner-friendly recipes, tips for creating juice blends, and answers to common juicing dilemmas.

As we start this journey, one crucial thing to remember is that juicing isn't a magic potion for instant health. While it's a fantastic way to boost your nutrient intake, it's not a substitute for a balanced and varied diet. Juicing should be viewed as a supplement to your diet, a way to add to the range of nutrients you consume.

Also, it's worth noting that while juicing provides a concentrated source of nutrients, it removes most of the fiber from fruits and vegetables. Hence, it's essential to continue to consume whole fruits and vegetables for their fiber content and other benefits.

Juicing is more than just a health fad; it's a lifestyle choice. It encourages a shift towards mindful eating, an appreciation for the natural flavors, and a deeper understanding of how different nutrients affect your body. Whether your motivation is to enhance your health, add a flavorful twist to your hydration, or experiment in your kitchen, juicing offers many benefits beyond the beverage in your glass.

So, let's begin this exciting journey together. Get ready to unlock a new world of flavors, nourish your body, and discover the joy and benefits of juicing.

Kara Kemp

Part 1: Why Juice: The Benefits of Juicing

Maintaining a balanced diet can be challenging in today's fast-paced society, where quick meals are often prioritized over nutritious ones. Enter juicing, a quick, easy, and delicious way to pack essential vitamins and minerals into your daily routine. But why should you juice? What are the benefits of this ever-growing trend?

Boosts Your Nutrient Intake

One of the main reasons people turn to juice is to increase their intake of essential nutrients. Fruits and vegetables are packed with vitamins, minerals, and antioxidants that your body needs to function optimally. Unfortunately, many people struggle to consume the recommended daily amount. Juicing provides a concentrated dose of these nutrients, enabling you to get your daily quota in just a glass or two.

Aids in Digestion

Juicing can also aid in digestion. We remove most of the fiber by extracting the juice from fruits and vegetables, leaving behind a liquid your body can digest more easily. This makes it an excellent option for those with sensitive digestive systems or conditions restricting their fiber intake.

Enhances Hydration

Although Water should always be your primary source of hydration, the water content in fresh juice also contributes to your daily fluid intake. Especially in warmer climates or during exercise, an extra boost of hydration can be beneficial.

Encourages Variety

Juicing encourages you to broaden your horizons regarding fruits and vegetables. It allows you to experiment with different combinations, helping to introduce a variety of produce into your diet. This is important because other fruits and vegetables contain different types and levels of nutrients.

Increases Energy Levels

Many people report feeling more energetic after incorporating fresh juice into their diets. This can be attributed to the high nutrient content in the liquid, which your body can quickly absorb, leading to a natural energy boost.

Promotes Healthy Eating Habits

Once you begin to experience the benefits of consuming more fruits and vegetables through juicing, it often influences other areas of your diet and lifestyle. It can be a stepping stone towards a healthier diet and lifestyle overall.

Supports Immune Function

Many fruits and vegetables are rich in nutrients like vitamin C, vitamin A, and antioxidants, vital in supporting the immune system. Regularly consuming fresh juice can help bolster your immune defenses.

Skin Health

The nutrients in juice – particularly antioxidants and vitamins like A, C, and E – can improve skin health, promoting a more vibrant complexion. Regularly drinking fresh juice may contribute to healthier, more radiant skin over time.

In conclusion, juicing can be a powerful tool to enhance your nutrient intake and overall health. However, remember that juicing should not be seen as a cure-all or replacement for a balanced diet. Instead, it should complement a diet rich in whole, unprocessed foods. Enjoy exploring the world of juicing, discovering new flavors, and reaping its many health benefits.

Kara Kemp

Part 2: Myth-Busting Common Misconceptions about Juicing

As juicing has grown in popularity, so too have misconceptions about this healthful practice. It's important to separate fact from fiction to approach juicing in a balanced and beneficial way. In this section, we'll debunk some common myths about juicing.

Myth 1: Juicing is a quick fix for weight loss

While juicing can help increase your nutrient intake and be part of a healthy, balanced diet, it is not a magic bullet for weight loss. Weight loss should come from a sustained calorie deficit, regular exercise, and a balanced diet. Juicing can be a part of this picture but should be seen as something other than a standalone solution.

Myth 2: Juicing is better than eating whole fruits and vegetables

Juicing provides a concentrated source of nutrients but removes the fiber found in whole fruits and vegetables. This fiber aids digestion, keeps you full, and has numerous other health benefits. Both whole fruits and vegetables and their juices have a place in a balanced diet.

Myth 3: All juices are created equal

Not all juices are nutritionally equal. Freshly made juices contain more nutrients than bottled juices, which often have added sugars and fewer vitamins due to pasteurization. It's also important to note that fruit juices are higher in sugars and should be balanced with vegetable juices.

5

Juicing for beginners

Myth 4: Green juice is the healthiest juice

While green juice from leafy vegetables like spinach and Kale is very healthy, that doesn't mean other fluids are not. Different colored fruits and vegetables provide various nutrients, so a rainbow-colored diet is the best approach to getting multiple vitamins and minerals.

Myth 5: Juicing detoxifies the body

Our bodies naturally detoxify through the liver, kidneys, and other systems. While a juice cleanser might help you feel better, eliminating processed foods and added sugars from your diet for a short period is unnecessary for 'detoxing.' The juice could do more harm than good by depriving your body of the necessary proteins and fats.

Myth 6: Juicing is too time-consuming

While juicing can take longer than grabbing pre-packaged juice, the benefits are well worth it. Juicers today are easy to use and clean, making them a manageable part of your daily routine. Plus, the taste of fresh juice is unrivaled!

Myth 7: Juicing is too expensive

While some fruits and vegetables can be pricey, plenty of affordable options are available. Also, consider the cost of health problems resulting from a poor diet. Investing in your health now could save you medical expenses in the future. And remember, you don't need to go organic on everything; focus on the 'Dirty Dozen' - a list of fruits and vegetables with the highest pesticide exposure.

By debunking these myths, we aim to provide a clear, balanced view of juicing. Enjoy the process of experimenting with flavors, discovering your favorites, and reaping the benefits of this nutrient-rich addition to your diet. Remember that moderation and variety are essential, as with everything in life!

Kara Kemp

Part 3: Understanding Your Equipment

DIFFERENT TYPES OF JUICERS

Choosing the right juicer can feel daunting, especially with the many types, brands, and models available. But worry not; this chapter aims to simplify the process by breaking down the main types of juicers you'll come across and their unique benefits.

There are three types of juicers: Centrifugal Juicers, Masticating Juicers (also known as Cold Press Juicers or Slow Juicers), and Triturating Juicers (Twin Gear Juicers).

Centrifugal Juicers

Centrifugal juicers are the most common type and are usually more affordable. They operate at high speed, using a sharp blade to chop the fruits and vegetables while a spinning filter separates the juice from the pulp.

BENEFITS:

- Fast juicing process.
- Typically more affordable.
- Easy to use and clean.

DRAWBACKS:

- Tend to be louder due to the high-speed motor.
- The heat produced by the high speed may reduce some nutrient content.
- Less efficient at juicing leafy greens and wheatgrass.

Masticating Juicers

Masticating juicers, also known as cold press or slow juicers, use a slow-moving auger to crush the fruits and vegetables against a stainless-steel mesh screen. This process extracts the juice, pushed through a narrow outlet into your glass, while the pulp is expelled separately.

BENEFITS:

- Operate quietly.
- More efficient at extracting juice, especially from leafy greens and wheatgrass.
- The slow speed produces less heat, preserving more nutrients.

DRAWBACKS:

- Typically more expensive.
- The juicing process is slower.

Triturating Juicers

Triturating juicers, also known as twin gear or double auger juicers, are the top-of-the-line in juicing machines. They use two gears that rotate inwards to crush and grind fruits and vegetables into excellent particles.

BENEFITS:

- Excellent juice yield.
- Minimal oxidation, preserving nutrients.
- Can juice a wide variety of produce, including leafy greens, wheatgrass, and even nuts for nut milk.

<u>DRAWBACKS</u>:

- Typically the most expensive option.
- More parts to clean.
- More time-consuming to use.

Choosing the right juicer depends on several factors, including your budget, what type of produce you plan on juicing most often, how vital nutrient preservation is to you, and how much time you're willing to spend on juicing and cleanup.

The right juicer can turn juicing from a chore into an enjoyable ritual. Remember, the best juicer for you is the one you'll enjoy using every day. The investment you make in your health will continue to pay dividends in the form of vibrant health and vitality.

Juicing for beginners

Part 4: Basic Recipes

GREEN JUICES RECIPES

Green juices are a fantastic way to consume essential vitamins and minerals, especially for those struggling to incorporate enough greens into their regular meals. Here are a few delectable green juice recipes with specific weight measurements and approximate calorie counts for precision and awareness of your calorie intake.

Remember, these are approximations, and actual calorie counts can vary depending on your produce's specific variety and ripeness.

GREEN DETOX DELIGHT

Weight: 1.3 kg   **Total Calorie Count: 349 Calories**

INGREDIENTS

- 200g Spinach (46 calories)
- 2 Medium Sized Apples (190 calories)
- 3 Medium Sized Carrots (75 calories)
- 1 Lemon (17 calories)
- 2 Stalks of Celery (12 calories)
- 1 Inch of Ginger Root (9 calories)
- 500ml Water (0 calories)

BENEFITS

This delightful blend is perfect for a detox. Spinach provides the necessary iron and calcium for healthy blood and bones. Apples boost your immune system with Vitamin C, while carrots supply a healthy dose of Vitamin A, promoting good vision. Celery, a natural diuretic, helps to reduce water retention and bloating. Ginger aids in digestion, adding a warming touch to the blend.

Kara Kemp

LEAFY GREEN GOODNESS

Weight: 1.1 kg   Total Calorie Count: 428 Calories

INGREDIENTS

- 300g Kale (150 calories)
- 2 Medium Sized Pears (204 calories)
- 1 Cucumber (45 calories)
- 1 Lime (20 calories)
- 1 Inch of Ginger Root (9 calories)
- 500ml Water (0 calories)

BENEFITS

Kale, the primary ingredient, is among the most nutrient-dense foods on the planet, loaded with antioxidants for protecting the body from harmful free radicals. Pears contribute additional fiber to keep you full longer. Cucumbers hydrate your body, and their mild flavor balances the more pungent taste of Kale and ginger.

SWEET AND ZESTY GREENS

Weight: 1.2 kg   Total Calorie Count: 615 Calories

INGREDIENTS

- 200g Romaine Lettuce (34 calories)
- 2 Medium Sized Pineapples (452 calories)
- 1 Medium Sized Cucumber (45 calories)
- 2 Medium Sized Kiwis (84 calories)
- 500ml Water (0 calories)

BENEFITS

Romaine lettuce, rich in vitamins A, C, and K, forms the base of this juice. Pineapples add a tropical sweetness and are packed with bromelain, an enzyme that helps with digestion and inflammation. Kiwis add a tangy touch and a significant amount of Vitamin C.

Juicing for beginners

POWER-PACKED GREENS

Weight: 1.4 kg **Total Calorie Count: 347 Calories**

INGREDIENTS

- 200g Spinach (46 calories)
- 200g Swiss Chard (70 calories)
- 2 Medium Sized Apples (190 calories)
- 1 Lemon (17 calories)
- 1 Inch of Turmeric Root (24 calories)
- 500ml Water (0 calories)

BENEFITS

Spinach and Swiss chard provide a high dose of iron and calcium. Apples add sweetness and an amount of Vitamin C, while lemon offers additional Vitamin C and aids digestion. Turmeric, known for its active compound curcumin, is a potent anti-inflammatory and antioxidant ingredient.

TROPICAL GREEN FUSION

Weight: 1.3 kg **Total Calorie Count: 627 Calories**

INGREDIENTS

- 200g Kale (150 calories)
- 1 Medium Sized Mango (201 calories)
- 2 Medium Sized Bananas (210 calories)
- 1 Lime (20 calories)
- 500ml Coconut Water (46 calories)

BENEFITS

This juice provides a real tropical treat. Kale brings nutrient-dense benefits, while Mango adds a sweet taste and a massive amount of Vitamin A. Bananas provide potassium, essential for heart health and normal blood pressure. Lime brightens the juice, and coconut water adds natural sweetness and excellent hydration.

CUCUMBER LEM

Weight: 1.1 kg   **Total Calorie Count: 342 Calories**

INGREDIENTS

- 3 Medium Sized Cucumbers (135 calories)
- 2 Green Apples (190 calories)
- 1 Lemon (17 calories)
- 500ml Water (0 calories)

BENEFITS

Cucumbers, which comprise the bulk of this juice, are highly hydrating, and their mild flavor provides a refreshing taste. Green apples add a dash of sweetness and a dose of Vitamin C, while lemon offers additional Vitamin C and aids digestion, creating a light and excellent juice perfect for a hot day.

TANGY GREENS

Weight: 1.3 kg   **Total Calorie Count: 285 Calories**

INGREDIENTS

- 200g Spinach (46 calories)
- 2 Medium Sized Green Apples (190 calories)
- 2 Limes (40 calories)
- 1 Inch of Ginger Root (9 calories)
- 500ml Water (0 calories)

BENEFITS

This juice is tangy and refreshing, thanks to the limes. Spinach provides the necessary iron and calcium for healthy blood and bones. Apples bring a dash of sweetness, and a boost of Vitamin C. Ginger aids digestion and adds a warming touch to the blend, resulting in a juice that's as revitalizing as it is tasty.

Juicing for beginners

MINTY FRESH FUSION

Weight: 1.2 kg   **Total Calorie Count: 400 Calories**

INGREDIENTS

- 200g Kale (150 calories)
- 1 Medium Sized Cucumber (45 calories)
- 2 Green Apples (190 calories)
- A Handful of Fresh Mint Leaves (15 calories)
- 500ml Water (0 calories)

BENEFITS

This recipe offers a refreshing and invigorating blend—the nutrient-rich kale pairs well with the hydrating cucumber. Green apples add sweetness, and a dose of Vitamin C. Mint leaves offer a fresh and aromatic twist while promoting good digestion.

CITRUS GREENS

Weight: 1.3 kg   **Total Calorie Count: 239 Calories**

INGREDIENTS

- 200g Spinach (46 calories)
- 1 Grapefruit (52 calories)
- 1 Lemon (17 calories)
- 2 Oranges (124 calories)
- 500ml Water (0 calories)

BENEFITS

This juice provides an excellent source of Vitamin C from the citrus fruits—grapefruit, lemon, and oranges—which can boost your immune system. Spinach provides necessary iron and calcium for healthy blood and bones, making this juice delicious and nutritious.

Kara Kemp

GREEN VEGGIE SURPRISE

Weight: 1.5 kg   **Total Calorie Count: 294 Calories**

INGREDIENTS

- 200g Kale (150 calories)
- 2 Medium Sized Carrots (75 calories)
- 1 Medium Sized Cucumber (45 calories)
- 1 Green Bell Pepper (24 calories)
- 500ml Water (0 calories)

BENEFITS

A surprise in every sip, this juice features green bell pepper for a unique twist. Kale, the primary ingredient, is packed with antioxidants, carrots provide Vitamin A. Cucumbers add hydration, and green bell pepper offers Vitamin C and a distinctive flavor profile.

APPLE AND CELERY BLEND

Weight: 1.2 kg   **Total Calorie Count: 254 Calories**

INGREDIENTS

- 200g Spinach (46 calories)
- 2 Green Apples (190 calories)
- 3 Stalks of Celery (18 calories)
- 500ml Water (0 calories)

BENEFITS

Simple yet delicious, this juice highlights the crisp flavors of apple and celery. Spinach provides iron and calcium, while apples add sweetness and Vitamin C. Celery contributes a unique taste and aids in hydration due to its high water content.

ZESTY GREEN CLEANSE

Weight: 1.3 kg | **Total Calorie Count: 307 Calories**

INGREDIENTS

- 200g Spinach (46 calories)
- 2 Medium Sized Green Apples (190 calories)
- 1 Medium Sized Cucumber (45 calories)
- 1 Lemon (17 calories)
- 1 Inch of Ginger Root (9 calories)
- 500ml Water (0 calories)

BENEFITS

This recipe features lemon and ginger, renowned for their cleansing properties. Spinach provides iron and calcium, while apples add sweetness and a dose of Vitamin C. Cucumbers hydrate your body, and their mild flavor balances the spicy taste of ginger and lemon.

THE GREEN BEET

Weight: 1.5 kg | **Total Calorie Count: 328 Calories**

INGREDIENTS

- 200g Kale (150 calories)
- 2 Medium Sized Beets (116 calories)
- 1 Medium Sized Cucumber (45 calories)
- 1 Lemon (17 calories)
- 500ml Water (0 calories)

BENEFITS

This juice is an excellent source of potassium, thanks to the beets, which also give the juice a beautiful color. Kale, packed with antioxidants, pairs well with the hydrating cucumber. Lemon offers additional Vitamin C and aids digestion, making this juice visually appealing and health-boosting.

Kara Kemp

MORNING GREEN GLORY

Weight: 1.4 kg | Total Calorie Count: 323 Calories

INGREDIENTS

- 200g Spinach (46 calories)
- 2 Medium Sized Green Apples (190 calories)
- 1 Medium Sized Carrot (25 calories)
- 1 Orange (62 calories)
- 500ml Water (0 calories)

BENEFITS

The perfect morning pick-me-up, this juice features oranges for a zesty wake-up call. Spinach provides essential minerals, while apples contribute sweetness and Vitamin C. Carrots boost Vitamin A, leading to a balanced, nutrient-rich start to your day.

THE GREEN HYDRATOR

Weight: 1.2 kg | Total Calorie Count: 182 Calories

INGREDIENTS

- 200g Romaine Lettuce (34 calories)
- 2 Medium Sized Cucumbers (90 calories)
- 2 Stalks of Celery (12 calories)
- 500ml Coconut Water (46 calories)

BENEFITS

A juice perfect for hydration, this recipe features cucumber, celery, and coconut water, all high in water content. Romaine lettuce adds a touch of green and a boost of vitamins A, C, and K. It's the ideal post-workout refresher or a midday pick-me-up.

GREEN POWERHOUSE

Weight: 1.6 kg   Total Calorie Count: 625 Calories

INGREDIENTS

- 200g Kale (150 calories)
- 2 Medium Sized Green Apples (190 calories)
- 1 Medium Sized Cucumber (45 calories)
- 1 Medium Sized Avocado (240 calories)
- 500ml Water (0 calories)

BENEFITS

This recipe features avocado, which adds a creamy texture and is an excellent source of healthy fats and fiber. One of the most nutrient-dense foods, Kale teams up with the hydrating cucumber. Apples add sweetness and a boost of Vitamin C, making this a juice that genuinely packs a punch.

GREEN ANTIOXIDANT BLEND

Weight: 1.3 kg   Total Calorie Count: 177 Calories

INGREDIENTS

- 200g Spinach (46 calories)
- 1 Medium Sized Cucumber (45 calories)
- 1 Cup of Blueberries (84 calories)
- 500ml Green Tea (2 calories)

BENEFITS

: An antioxidant powerhouse, this recipe features blueberries and green tea, known for their high antioxidant content. Spinach provides iron and calcium, and cucumber adds hydration, creating a balanced blend for skin health and overall wellness.

Kara Kemp

VITAMIN C BOOSTER

Weight: 1.2 kg | Total Calorie Count: 300 Calories

INGREDIENTS

- 200g Kale (150 calories)
- 2 Medium Sized Oranges (124 calories)
- 1 Lemon (17 calories)
- 1 Inch of Ginger Root (9 calories)
- 500ml Water (0 calories)

BENEFITS

This juice contains Vitamin C from oranges and lemons, boosting your immune system. Kale brings in a healthy dose of iron, while ginger adds a touch of warmth and aids digestion, making this a tangy, refreshing, and nutrient-packed juice.

GREEN APPLE CRISP

Weight: 1.3 kg | Total Calorie Count: 348 Calories

INGREDIENTS

- 200g Spinach (46 calories)
- 3 Medium Sized Green Apples (285 calories)
- 1 Lemon (17 calories)
- 500ml Water (0 calories)

BENEFITS

: The star of this recipe, green apple, offers a crisp flavor and a solid dose of Vitamin C. Spinach contributes necessary iron and calcium for healthy blood and bones. Lemon gives an extra kick of Vitamin C and aids digestion, making this a simple, sweet, and refreshing blend.

Juicing for beginners

TROPICAL GREEN DELIGHT

Weight: 1.5 kg   **Total Calorie Count: 377 Calories**

INGREDIENTS

- 200g Spinach (46 calories)
- 2 Medium Sized Kiwis (84 calories)
- 1 Medium Sized Mango (201 calories)
- 500ml Coconut Water (46 calories)

BENEFITS

This tropical juice contains vitamin C from the kiwis and Mango, and spinach provides necessary iron and calcium. Coconut water adds natural sweetness and hydration, making this juice a delightful, exotic treat.

SPICY GREEN REFRESHER

Weight: 1.2 kg   **Total Calorie Count: 273 Calories**

INGREDIENTS

- 200g Romaine Lettuce (34 calories)
- 1 Medium Sized Cucumber (45 calories)
- 2 Medium Sized Green Apples (190 calories)
- 1 Jalapeno Pepper (4 calories)
- 500ml Water (0 calories)

BENEFITS

Jalapeno peppers spice up this juice, giving it a surprising kick. Romaine lettuce provides vitamins A, C, and K, while cucumber and apples add hydration and sweetness. This juice is a bold blend of refreshing and spicy.

Kara Kemp

THE GREEN WARRIOR

Weight: 1.4 kg   Total Calorie Count: 330 Calories

INGREDIENTS

- 200g Spinach (46 calories)
- 1 Medium Sized Cucumber (45 calories)
- 1 Medium Sized Carrot (25 calories)
- 2 Medium Sized Green Apples (190 calories)
- 1 Inch of Turmeric Root (24 calories)
- 500ml Water (0 calories)

BENEFITS

This juice is a true warrior, packed with nutrients and antioxidants. Turmeric, known for its anti-inflammatory benefits, combines iron-rich spinach, hydrating cucumber, vitamin A-rich carrots, and vitamin C-rich apples to make a robust and health-boosting juice.

GINGER GREEN ZING

Weight: 1.2 kg   Total Calorie Count: 363 Calories

INGREDIENTS

- 200g Kale (150 calories)
- 2 Medium Sized Pears (204 calories)
- 1 Inch of Ginger Root (9 calories)
- 500ml Water (0 calories)

BENEFITS

This juice has a zingy kick from the ginger, which also aids in digestion. Kale provides a healthy dose of iron, and pears add sweetness and fiber, making this a delicious and satisfying juice blend.

Juicing for beginners

Part 4: Basic Recipes

FRUIT JUICES

Fruit juices are an excellent way to consume essential nutrients while enjoying many refreshing flavors. Suppose you are conscious about your calorie intake or want to get precise with your juicing quantities. This section provides several delicious fruit juice recipes with specific weight measurements and approximate calorie counts.

Note that these calorie estimates may vary slightly based on your fruits' variety and ripeness.

TROPICAL SUNRISE

Weight: 1.3 kg   Total Calorie Count: 777 Calories

INGREDIENTS

- 2 Medium Sized Oranges (124 calories)
- 1 Medium Sized Pineapple (452 calories)
- 1 Medium Sized Mango (201 calories)
- 500ml Water (0 calories)

BENEFITS

This juice brings a taste of the tropics, with Vitamin C-packed oranges, pineapple for a blast of bromelain enzyme, which aids in digestion, and Mango for extra sweetness and Vitamin A. This delightful blend is perfect for a sunny morning pick-me-up.

Kara Kemp

BERRY ANTIOXIDANT BLAST

Weight: 1.2 kg

Total Calorie Count: 202 Calories

INGREDIENTS

- 1 Cup of Strawberries (53 calories)
- 1 Cup of Blueberries (84 calories)
- 1 Cup of Raspberries (65 calories)
- 500ml Water (0 calories)

BENEFITS

This juice is a berry lovers' delight, packed with antioxidants from strawberries, blueberries, and raspberries. The berries also provide significant Vitamin C and fiber, making this juice a delicious and healthy treat.

SWEET CITRUS SYMPHONY

Weight: 1.2 kg

Total Calorie Count: 323 Calories

INGREDIENTS

- 2 Medium Sized Oranges (124 calories)
- 2 Medium Sized Grapefruits (182 calories)
- 1 Lemon (17 calories)
- 500ml Water (0 calories)

BENEFITS

This juice features a symphony of citrus, providing an impressive amount of Vitamin C, which is known to boost the immune system. Grapefruits add a distinctive tangy sweetness and are known to aid in weight loss and promote healthy skin.

APPLE PEAR DELIGHT

Weight: 1.2 kg   Total Calorie Count: 498 Calories

INGREDIENTS

- 3 Medium Sized Green Apples (285 calories)
- 2 Medium Sized Pears (204 calories)
- 1 Inch of Ginger Root (9 calories)
- 500ml Water (0 calories)

BENEFITS

Apples and pears make this juice delightfully sweet, and both fruits are excellent sources of dietary fiber. Ginger adds a zing and aids digestion, making this juice tasty and beneficial for gut health.

MELON REFRESH

Weight: 1.5 kg   Total Calorie Count: 549 Calories

INGREDIENTS

- Half of a Watermelon (455 calories)
- Half of a Cantaloupe (94 calories)
- 500ml Water (0 calories)

BENEFITS

This juice is highly hydrating due to the high water content of watermelon and cantaloupe. Both fruits are also packed with Vitamins A and C. This juice is perfect for quenching your thirst on a hot day and boosting your skin health with its vitamin content.

Kara Kemp

MANGO TANGO

Weight: 1.3 kg   **Total Calorie Count: 492 Calories**

INGREDIENTS

- 3 Medium Sized Green Apples (285 calories)
- 2 Medium Sized Pears (204 calories)
- 1 Inch of Ginger Root (9 calories)
- 500ml Water (0 calories)

BENEFITS

Mango Tango is a sweet, tropical delight. Mangoes are high in vitamins C, A, and fiber, boosting your immune system, promoting eye health, and aiding digestion. Pineapple contains:

·Bromelain.

·An enzyme is known for its anti-inflammatory and digestion-aiding properties.

·Making this juice beneficial for digestion and overall well-being.

BERRY MELON BLEND

Weight: 1.4 kg   **Total Calorie Count: 388 Calories**

INGREDIENTS

- 700g Watermelon (210 calories)
- 200g Blueberries (114 calories)
- 200g Strawberries (64 calories)
- 500ml Water (0 calories)

BENEFITS

Berry Melon Blend combines the hydrating properties of watermelon with the antioxidant benefits of blueberries and strawberries. Watermelon, high in water content and essential hydration, is perfect for hot days. The berries are rich in antioxidants, which fight off harmful free radicals, and are high in vitamin C, known to enhance immunity.

Juicing for beginners

CITRUS GINGER ZING

Weight: 1.2 kg   **Total Calorie Count: 356 Calories**

INGREDIENTS

- 300g Oranges (153 calories)
- 400g Grapefruits (154 calories)
- 100g Lemon (29 calories)
- 25g Ginger Root (20 calories)
- 500ml Water (0 calories)

BENEFITS

Citrus Ginger Zing is a refreshing blend with a vitamin C boost from citrus fruits and digestion-aiding benefits from ginger. This juice is a great way to support your immune system and promote gut health. Additionally, ginger has anti-inflammatory properties, which can benefit people with arthritis or other inflammatory conditions.

PEACHY KEEN

Weight: 1.3 kg   **Total Calorie Count: 430 Calories**

INGREDIENTS

- 500g Peaches (190 calories)
- 400g Pears (240 calories)
- 500ml Water (0 calories)

BENEFITS

Peachy Keen is a light, nutritious juice option high in vitamins and minerals. Peaches and pears contain dietary fiber and a range of vitamins and minerals. They are also low in calories and high in Water, making this juice hydrating and beneficial for weight management and digestion.

Kara Kemp

TROPICAL GREEN DREAM

Weight: 1.4 kg   **Total Calorie Count: 483 Calories**

INGREDIENTS

- 300g Kiwis (183 calories)
- 400g Pineapple (200 calories)
- 500ml Coconut Water (100 calories)

BENEFITS

Tropical Green Dream is a tropical, refreshing juice rich in vitamins and electrolytes. Kiwis are a great vitamin C and dietary fiber source, promoting a healthy immune system and gut health. Pineapple provides the digestion-aiding enzyme bromelain, while coconut water is rich in electrolytes, making this juice hydrating and beneficial for digestion and overall wellness.

APPLE BERRY BLAST

Weight: 1.3 kg   **Total Calorie Count: 494 Calories**

INGREDIENTS

- 500g Green Apples (260 calories)
- 200g Blueberries (114 calories)
- 200g Raspberries (120 calories)
- 500ml Water (0 calories)

BENEFITS

Apple Berry Blast is full of sweet flavors and vital nutrients. Green apples are high in dietary fiber and vitamin C, promoting a healthy gut and immune system. Blueberries and raspberries are known for their antioxidant properties, helping to combat oxidative stress in the body. This juice is an excellent choice for a health-boosting, delicious beverage.

RADIANT RUBY

Weight: 1.3 kg	Total Calorie Count: 608 Calories

INGREDIENTS

- 500g Pomegranate seeds (332 calories)
- 400g Red Grapes (276 calories)
- 500ml Water (0 calories)

BENEFITS

Radiant Ruby juice is a rich source of antioxidants and vitamins. Pomegranates are known for their antioxidant properties, helping to combat oxidative stress in the body. Red grapes are a good source of vitamins K and C, which are essential for bone health and immunity. This juice is a refreshing, health-boosting beverage.

SUNNY SPLASH

Weight: 1.2 kg	Total Calorie Count: 465 Calories

INGREDIENTS

- 500g Oranges (245 calories)
- 200g Pineapple (100 calories)
- 200g Papaya (120 calories)
- 500ml Water (0 calories)

BENEFITS

Sunny Splash is a vibrant tropical delight loaded with vitamin C from oranges and pineapple, which supports a healthy immune system. The papaya adds a healthy dose of fiber and a digestive enzyme called papain, making this juice excellent for digestion and overall well-being.

Kara Kemp

CRIMSON CRUSH

Weight: 1.4 kg　　　　**Total Calorie Count: 368 Calories**

INGREDIENTS

- 500g Red Plums (240 calories)
- 400g Strawberries (128 calories)
- 500ml Water (0 calories)

BENEFITS

Crimson Crush is a sweet and tangy blend packed with antioxidants from both plums and strawberries. This juice provides a high dose of vitamin C, which supports the immune system and promotes skin health.

SUMMER BREEZE

Weight: 1.4 kg　　　　**Total Calorie Count: 418 Calories**

INGREDIENTS

- 500g Cantaloupe (170 calories)
- 400g Kiwi (248 calories)
- 500ml Water (0 calories)

BENEFITS

Summer Breeze is a sweet, refreshing juice high in vitamins A and C from the cantaloupe and kiwi, promoting eye health and boosting the immune system. The high water content of cantaloupe adds to its hydrating properties, making it an excellent choice for hot summer days.

BANANA BERRY DELIGHT

Weight: 1.4 kg   **Total Calorie Count: 594 Calories**

INGREDIENTS

- 400g Bananas (360 calories)
- 200g Blueberries (114 calories)
- 200g Raspberries (120 calories)
- 500ml Water (0 calories)

BENEFITS

Banana Berry Delight is a creamy, sweet juice rich in vitamins, minerals, and antioxidants. Bananas provide potassium and vitamin B6, supporting heart health and brain function, while blueberries and raspberries offer potent antioxidants that fight free radicals.

PEAR PLEASURE

Weight: 1.3 kg   **Total Calorie Count: 456 Calories**

INGREDIENTS

- 600g Pears (360 calories)
- 200g Blackberries (96 calories)
- 500ml Water (0 calories)

BENEFITS

Pear Pleasure is a subtly sweet juice high in dietary fiber from pears and blackberries, promoting digestive health. Additionally, blackberries are packed with vitamins C and K, supporting immunity and helping with blood clotting. This juice is a beautiful option for a healthful, delicious beverage.

Kara Kemp

CITRUS SYMPHONY

Weight: 1.2 kg   **Total Calorie Count: 600 Calories**

INGREDIENTS

- 400g Oranges (196 calories)
- 400g Grapefruit (192 calories)
- 400g Tangerines (212 calories)

BENEFITS

Citrus Symphony is a tart and refreshing juice rich in vitamin C from various citrus fruits. This juice promotes immune health, skin health and hydrates due to the high water content in the fruits.

TROPICAL TWIST

Weight: 1.3 kg   **Total Calorie Count: 650 Calories**

INGREDIENTS

- 500g Pineapple (250 calories)
- 300g Mango (180 calories)
- 500g Papaya (220 calories)

BENEFITS

Tropical Twist is a sweet, tropical delight rich in vitamin C and dietary fiber from pineapple, Mango, and papaya. This juice promotes a healthy immune system, supports digestion, and provides a healthy dose of antioxidants.

BERRY BONANZA

Weight: 1.2 kg	Total Calorie Count: 548 Calories

INGREDIENTS

- 400g Strawberries (128 calories)
- 400g Blueberries (228 calories)
- 400g Blackberries (192 calories)

BENEFITS

Berry Bonanza is a sweet-tart juice packed with antioxidants from strawberries, blueberries, and blackberries. This juice is excellent for fighting free radicals, supporting immune health, and promoting skin health.

AUTUMN DELIGHT

Weight: 1.3 kg	Total Calorie Count: 728 Calories

INGREDIENTS

- 650g Apples (338 calories)
- 650g Pears (390 calories)

BENEFITS

Autumn Delight is a sweet, subtly tart juice rich in dietary fiber from apples and pears. This juice promotes digestive health, offers a moderate dose of vitamin C, and is a comforting, healthful beverage option.

Kara Kemp

SUNSET BLEND

Weight: 1.2 kg   Total Calorie Count: 564 Calories

INGREDIENTS

- 400g Peaches (152 calories)
- 400g Apricots (192 calories)
- 400g Nectarines (220 calories)

BENEFITS

Sunset Blend is a sweet, tangy juice rich in vitamins A and C from peaches, apricots, and nectarines. This juice promotes skin health, eye health, and a healthy immune system.

GRAPEFUL BLISS

Weight: 1.3 kg   Total Calorie Count: 728 Calories

INGREDIENTS

- 650g Red Grapes (348 calories)
- 650g Green Grapes (380 calories)

BENEFITS

Grapeful Bliss is a refreshing juice with antioxidants, especially resveratrol from red grapes. This juice promotes heart health and offers a range of vitamins and minerals.

Juicing for beginners

MELON MEDLEY

Weight: 1.6 kg   **Total Calorie Count: 528 Calories**

INGREDIENTS

- 800g Watermelon (240 calories)
- 400g Honeydew (152 calories)
- 400g Cantaloupe (136 calories)

BENEFITS

Melon Medley is a hydrating, refreshing juice high in vitamins A and C from watermelon, honeydew, and cantaloupe. This juice promotes hydration, skin health, and a healthy immune system.

KIWI BERRY BLAST

Weight: 1.2 kg   **Total Calorie Count: 564 Calories**

INGREDIENTS

- 400g Kiwi (244 calories)
- 400g Strawberries (128 calories)
- 400g Raspberries (192 calories)

BENEFITS

Kiwi Berry Blast is a tart, sweet juice high in vitamin C and antioxidants from kiwi, strawberries, and raspberries. This juice promotes immune health, fights free radicals, and supports digestive health due to its high fiber content.

Kara Kemp

Part 4: Basic Recipes

ROOT VEGETABLE JUICES

Root vegetables are packed with a variety of essential nutrients and antioxidants. Juicing these nutrient powerhouses can provide an excellent way to incorporate these valuable foods into your diet easily. The following recipes include specific weight measurements and approximate calorie counts to help you precisely plan your juices.

Remember, these calorie counts are approximations, and actual values may vary slightly depending on your produce's specific variety and ripeness.

CARROT KICK

Weight: 1.5 kg   Total Calorie Count: 450 Calories

INGREDIENTS

- 700g Carrots (294 calories)
- 300g Apples (156 calories)
- 500ml Water (0 calories)

BENEFITS

Carrot Kick is a sweet, earthy juice rich in beta-carotene from carrots, which is converted into vitamin A in your body. This juice promotes eye health, skin health, and a healthy immune system. Adding apples provides a refreshing sweetness and additional vitamin C for an immune boost.

BEETROOT BLISS

Weight: 1.2 kg   **Total Calorie Count: 450 Calories**

INGREDIENTS

- 600g Beetroot (252 calories)
- 300g Cucumbers (45 calories)
- 300g Oranges (153 calories)

BENEFITS

Beetroot Bliss is a sweet, earthy juice with the added freshness of cucumber and oranges. Beetroot is known for its ability to help lower blood pressure and enhance athletic performance due to its high nitrate content. Oranges add a vitamin C boost, promoting immune health.

SWEET POTATO POWER

Weight: 1.5 kg   **Total Calorie Count: 660 Calories**

INGREDIENTS

- 500g Sweet Potatoes (430 calories)
- 300g Carrots (126 calories)
- 200g Apples (104 calories)
- 500ml Water (0 calories)

BENEFITS

: Sweet Potato Power is a unique, sweet juice high in beta-carotene from sweet potatoes and carrots. This juice promotes eye health, skin health, and a healthy immune system. Apples add a touch of sweetness and an extra dose of fiber and vitamin C.

RADISH REVIVE

Weight: 1 kg **Total Calorie Count: 315 Calories**

INGREDIENTS

- 500g Radishes (80 calories)
- 250g Carrots (105 calories)
- 250g Apples (130 calories)

BENEFITS

Radish Revive is a peppery, earthy juice with apple sweetness. Radishes are known for their detoxifying properties and their ability to aid digestion. Carrots add a dose of beta-carotene, promoting eye health and boosting the immune system.

GINGER GLOW

Weight: 1.5 kg **Total Calorie Count: 478 Calories**

INGREDIENTS

- 700g Carrots (294 calories)
- 100g Ginger Root (80 calories)
- 200g Apples (104 calories)
- 500ml Water (0 calories)

BENEFITS

Ginger Glow is a spicy, sweet, earthy juice packed with nutrients. Carrots provide a large amount of beta-carotene, promoting eye health, while ginger adds a potent anti-inflammatory kick and aids in digestion. Apples add a refreshing sweetness and a touch of vitamin C for an immune boost.

PARSNIP PLEASURE

Weight: 1.2 kg   Total Calorie Count: 674 Calories

INGREDIENTS

- 500g Parsnips (350 calories)
- 300g Apples (156 calories)
- 400g Carrots (168 calories)

BENEFITS

Parsnip Pleasure is a sweet and slightly spicy juice rich in vitamins C and E from parsnips and carrots. It promotes a healthy immune system and skin health and has anti-inflammatory properties. Apples add a refreshing sweetness and additional vitamin C.

TURNIP TANGO

Weight: 1 kg   Total Calorie Count: 408 Calories

INGREDIENTS

- 500g Turnips (173 calories)
- 250g Apples (130 calories)
- 250g Carrots (105 calories)

BENEFITS

Turnip Tango is an earthy juice with a sweet finish from the apples. Turnips are a great source of vitamin C and B6, promoting a healthy immune system and brain function. Carrots add a dose of beta-carotene, promoting eye health.

Kara Kemp

SPICY CELERIAC SOOTHER

Weight: 1.3 kg   Total Calorie Count: 392 Calories

INGREDIENTS

- 600g Celeriac (204 calories)
- 200g Apples (104 calories)
- 200g Carrots (84 calories)
- 300ml Water (0 calories)

BENEFITS

Spicy Celeriac Soother is an earthy, slightly spicy juice with sweetness from apples. Celeriac is high in vitamin K, promoting bone health, and has a high fiber content that supports digestion. Carrots add a beta-carotene boost, promoting eye health.

JICAMA JOY

Weight: 1.4 kg   Total Calorie Count: 459 Calories

INGREDIENTS

- 700g Jicama (274 calories)
- 350g Pears (185 calories)
- 350ml Water (0 calories)

BENEFITS

Jicama Joy is a slightly sweet, refreshing juice. Jicama is a fantastic fiber and vitamin C source, promoting a healthy immune system and aiding digestion. Pears add extra fiber and natural sweetness to this hydrating juice.

Juicing for beginners

FENNEL FRESH

Weight: 1.1 kg   **Total Calorie Count: 347 Calories**

INGREDIENTS

- 500g Fennel (146 calories)
- 300g Apples (156 calories)
- 300g Cucumbers (45 calories)

BENEFITS

Fennel Fresh is a light, refreshing juice with a unique taste from fennel. Fennel is known for its digestive uses and its source of vitamin C, promoting a healthy immune system. Apples add a refreshing sweetness, and cucumbers contribute to hydration.

RUTABAGA REVITALIZER

Weight: 1.1 kg   **Total Calorie Count: 467 Calories**

INGREDIENTS

- 500g Rutabaga (185 calories)
- 300g Apples (156 calories)
- 300g Carrots (126 calories)

BENEFITS

Rutabaga Revitalizer is an earthy juice with a sweetness from apples. Rutabaga is an excellent source of vitamin C and fiber, promoting a healthy immune system and aiding digestion. Carrots add a dose of beta-carotene, promoting eye health.

Kara Kemp

YAM YUM

Weight: 1.1 kg   **Total Calorie Count: 713 Calories**

INGREDIENTS

- 500g Yams (431 calories)
- 300g Apples (156 calories)
- 300g Carrots (126 calories)

BENEFITS

Yam Yum is a sweet and earthy juice, rich in vitamins C and A from yams and carrots. These nutrients help boost the immune system, promote skin health, and support good vision. Apples add a refreshing sweetness and an additional boost of vitamin C.

DAIKON DELIGHT

Weight: 1 kg   **Total Calorie Count: 326 Calories**

INGREDIENTS

- 500g Daikon Radish (91 calories)
- 250g Apples (130 calories)
- 250g Carrots (105 calories)

BENEFITS

Daikon Delight is a slightly spicy, earthy juice with a touch of sweetness from apples. Daikon radishes are known for their digestive benefits and their ability to detoxify the body. Carrots add a dose of beta-carotene, promoting eye health.

Juicing for beginners

GINGERED BEET

Weight: 1.2 kg   Total Calorie Count: 600 Calories

INGREDIENTS

- 500g Beetroots (210 calories)
- 300g Carrots (126 calories)
- 200g Apples (104 calories)
- 200g Ginger Root (160 calories)

BENEFITS

Gingered Beet is a sweet, earthy juice with a spicy kick from ginger. Beetroots are known for their ability to help lower blood pressure and enhance athletic performance. Carrots add a dose of beta-carotene, promoting eye health, and ginger aids in digestion and provide anti-inflammatory benefits.

ROOT MIX MEDLEY

Weight: 1.2 kg   Total Calorie Count: 514 Calories

INGREDIENTS

- 300g Carrots (126 calories)
- 300g Beetroots (126 calories)
- 300g Turnips (105 calories)
- 300g Parsnips (157 calories)

BENEFITS

Root Mix Medley is a deeply earthy juice combining the best of root vegetables. This nutrient-dense blend offers vitamins A, C, and E and promotes a healthy immune system, eye health, and good brain function.

Kara Kemp

ZESTY CELERY ROOT

Weight: 1.1 kg   **Total Calorie Count: 457 Calories**

INGREDIENTS

- 500g Celery Root (175 calories)
- 300g Apples (156 calories)
- 300g Carrots (126 calories)

BENEFITS

Zesty Celery Root is a tangy, earthy juice with a touch of sweetness from apples. Celery root is high in vitamin K and fiber, promoting bone health and aiding digestion. Carrots add a dose of beta-carotene, promoting eye health.

SALSIFY SURGE

Weight: 1.1 kg   **Total Calorie Count: 673 Calories**

INGREDIENTS

- 500g Salsify (325 calories)
- 300g Apples (156 calories)
- 300g Pears (192 calories)

BENEFITS

Salsify Surge is a sweet, slightly nutty juice. Salsify is a great source of fiber and vitamins C and B6, promoting a healthy immune system and aiding digestion. Apples and pears add a refreshing sweetness and an extra dose of fiber.

Juicing for beginners

KOHLRABI KICKSTART

Weight: 1.2 kg   **Total Calorie Count: 499 Calories**

INGREDIENTS

- 500g Kohlrabi (165 calories)
- 400g Apples (208 calories)
- 300g Carrots (126 calories)

BENEFITS

Kohlrabi Kickstart is a slightly sweet, mild juice with a pleasant earthiness. Kohlrabi is high in fiber and vitamin C, promoting a healthy immune system and aiding digestion. Carrots add a dose of beta-carotene, promoting eye health.

JERUSALEM ARTICHOKE JUICE

Weight: 1.1 kg   **Total Calorie Count: 680 Calories**

INGREDIENTS

- 500g Jerusalem Artichokes (398 calories)
- 300g Apples (156 calories)
- 300g Carrots (126 calories)

BENEFITS

Jerusalem Artichoke Juice is a mildly sweet and nutty juice. Jerusalem artichokes are high in inulin, a prebiotic that aids in gut health and also provides potassium. Carrots add a dose of beta-carotene, promoting eye health.

Kara Kemp

RADISH RUBY

Weight: 1 kg   **Total Calorie Count: 347 Calories**

INGREDIENTS

- 500g Radishes (87 calories)
- 500g Apples (260 calories)

BENEFITS

Radish Ruby is a peppery, slightly sweet juice. Radishes are known for supporting healthy digestion and detoxifying the body. Apples add a refreshing sweetness and a boost of vitamin C to help support a healthy immune system.

TURMERIC TONIC

Weight: 1.2 kg   **Total Calorie Count: 656 Calories**

INGREDIENTS

- 400g Carrots (168 calories)
- 200g Apples (104 calories)
- 200g Turmeric Root (192 calories)
- 400g Oranges (192 calories)

BENEFITS

Turmeric Tonic is a spicy, earthy juice with a sweet undertone. Turmeric is known for its anti-inflammatory properties and the ability to boost the immune system. Carrots provide beta-carotene, promoting eye health, while oranges add vitamin C for an immune boost.

LOTUS ROOT LUSTER

Weight: 1 kg | Total Calorie Count: 628 Calories

INGREDIENTS

- 500g Lotus Roots (350 calories)
- 250g Apples (130 calories)
- 250g Pears (148 calories)

BENEFITS

Lotus Root Luster is a subtly sweet, mildly earthy juice. Lotus roots are known for their high dietary fiber and vitamin C content, promoting a healthy immune system and aiding digestion. Apples and pears add a refreshing sweetness and an extra dose of fiber.

TARO TONIC

Weight: 1.2 kg | Total Calorie Count: 734 Calories

INGREDIENTS

- 500g Taro (552 calories)
- 350g Apples (182 calories)
- 350ml Water (0 calories)

BENEFITS

Taro Tonic is a mildly sweet, earthy juice. Taro is a good source of fiber and vitamins E and B6, promoting good brain function and healthy skin. Apples add a refreshing sweetness and an additional boost of vitamin C.

Kara Kemp

CASSAVA CURE

Weight: 1.3 kg   **Total Calorie Count: 767 Calories**

INGREDIENTS

- 500g Cassava (559 calories)
- 400g Apples (208 calories)
- 400ml Water (0 calories)

BENEFITS

Cassava Cure is a mildly sweet, earthy juice. Cassava is a good vitamin C and fiber source, promoting a healthy immune system and aiding digestion. Apples add a refreshing sweetness and an additional boost of vitamin C.

HORSERADISH HEAT

Weight: 1 kg   **Total Calorie Count: 575 Calories**

INGREDIENTS

- 300g Horseradish (246 calories)
- 350g Apples (182 calories)
- 350g Carrots (147 calories)

BENEFITS

Horseradish Heat is a spicy, earthy juice with a sweet undertone. Horseradish is known for stimulating digestion and boosting the immune system. Carrots provide beta-carotene, promoting eye health, while apples add a refreshing sweetness.

Juicing for beginners

Part 4: Basic Recipes

COMBO BLENDS

When it comes to juicing, combination juices offer the best of all worlds. These blends incorporate fruits, vegetables, and sometimes even herbs and spices, allowing you to enjoy a wider variety of flavors and nutritional benefits in a single glass. Below are a few combo blend recipes with specific weight measurements and approximate calorie counts for those interested in precision and keeping track of their calorie intake.

Please note that these calorie counts are estimations, and actual values can differ slightly based on your produce's specific variety and ripeness.

SUNNY START

Weight: 1 kg   Total Calorie Count: 450 Calories

INGREDIENTS

- 500g Oranges (240 calories)
- 500g Carrots (210 calories)

BENEFITS

Sunny Start is a sweet juice rich in vitamins C and A from oranges and carrots. It helps boost the immune system, promotes skin health, and supports good vision.

TROPICAL TANGO

Weight: 1.1 kg   **Total Calorie Count: 509 Calories**

INGREDIENTS

- 400g Pineapples (200 calories)
- 400g Mangoes (240 calories)
- 300g Spinach (69 calories)

BENEFITS

Tropical Tango is a sweet, tropical juice with a hint of earthiness from spinach. It contains vitamins C and A from fruits and spinach, promoting a healthy immune system and good vision.

GREEN POWER

Weight: 1.2 kg   **Total Calorie Count: 456 Calories**

INGREDIENTS

- 400g Cucumbers (48 calories)
- 400g Apples (208 calories)
- 400g Kale (200 calories)

BENEFITS

Green Power is a refreshing juice packed with vitamins K, C and A from kale and cucumber. It supports bone health, aids digestion, and promotes skin health.

Juicing for beginners

BERRY BEETS

Weight: 1 kg   **Total Calorie Count: 485 Calories**

INGREDIENTS

- 500g Beetroots (210 calories)
- 500g Mixed Berries (275 calories)

BENEFITS

Berry Beets are a sweet and earthy juice, rich in antioxidants from the mixed berries, and beneficial for heart health due to the beetroots.

PEACHY CLEAN

Weight: 1.1 kg   **Total Calorie Count: 441 Calories**

INGREDIENTS

- 600g Peaches (231 calories)
- 500g Carrots (210 calories)

BENEFITS

Peachy Clean is a sweet, refreshing juice. Peaches offer a good vitamin C and fiber source, promoting a healthy immune system and aiding digestion. Carrots add a dose of beta-carotene, promoting eye health.

Kara Kemp

AUTUMN SPICE

Weight: 1.2 kg | Total Calorie Count: 503 Calories

INGREDIENTS

- 500g Apples (260 calories)
- 400g Carrots (168 calories)
- 300g Pumpkin (75 calories)

BENEFITS

Autumn Spice is a warm, sweet juice. Apples offer a good source of vitamin C and fiber, promoting a healthy immune system and aiding digestion. Carrots and pumpkins add a good dose of beta-carotene, promoting eye health.

CELERY CITRUS

Weight: 1.1 kg | Total Calorie Count: 300 Calories

INGREDIENTS

- 600g Celery (60 calories)
- 500g Oranges (240 calories)

BENEFITS

Celery Citrus is a refreshing, slightly tangy juice. Celery is rich in vitamin K, promoting bone health. Oranges provide a good source of vitamin C, enabling a healthy immune system.

Juicing for beginners

PARSNIP PINEAPPLE

Weight: 1.2 kg   **Total Calorie Count: 700 Calories**

INGREDIENTS

- 500g Parsnips (350 calories)
- 700g Pineapples (350 calories)

BENEFITS

Parsnip Pineapple is a sweet, slightly spicy juice. Parsnips provide a good vitamin C and fiber source, promoting a healthy immune system and aiding digestion. Pineapple adds tropical sweetness and digestive benefits.

GINGERED GRAPEFRUIT

Weight: 1.1 kg   **Total Calorie Count: 568 Calories**

INGREDIENTS

- 500g Grapefruits (200 calories)
- 400g Apples (208 calories)
- 200g Ginger Root (160 calories)

BENEFITS

Gingered Grapefruit is a tangy, slightly spicy juice. Grapefruits are high in vitamins A and C, promoting skin health and a healthy immune system. Ginger adds a spicy kick and aids in digestion.

Kara Kemp

CUCUMBER CANTALOUPE

Weight: 1.1 kg   Total Calorie Count: 260 Calories

INGREDIENTS

- 600g Cantaloupe (180 calories)
- 500g Cucumbers (80 calories)

BENEFITS

Cucumber Cantaloupe is a sweet, refreshing juice. Cantaloupes are rich in vitamins A and C, promoting skin health and a healthy immune system. Cucumbers add extra hydration and vitamin K, promoting bone health.

WATERMELON WONDER

Weight: 1.5 kg   Total Calorie Count: 572 Calories

INGREDIENTS

- 1.3 kg Watermelon (468 calories)
- 200g Mint (104 calories)

BENEFITS

Watermelon Wonder is a hydrating, refreshing juice. Watermelon is high in vitamins A and C and hydrating. Mint adds a refreshing twist and aids in digestion.

Juicing for beginners

SUNRISE SMOOTHIE

Weight: 1.2 kg	Total Calorie Count: 488 Calories

INGREDIENTS

- 400g Oranges (192 calories)
- 400g Strawberries (128 calories)
- 400g Carrots (168 calories)

BENEFITS

Sunrise Smoothie is a sweet, vibrant juice packed with vitamins C and A, promoting a healthy immune system, good vision, and skin health.

RADIANT RADISH

Weight: 1 kg	Total Calorie Count: 337 Calories

INGREDIENTS

- 500g Radishes (87 calories)
- 500g Pineapples (250 calories)

BENEFITS

Radiant Radish is a peppery, slightly sweet juice. Radishes support healthy digestion and detoxification. Pineapples add tropical sweetness and digestive benefits.

Kara Kemp

GREEN APPLE GLORY

Weight: 1.2 kg   Total Calorie Count: 450 Calories

INGREDIENTS

- 600g Apples (312 calories)
- 600g Spinach (138 calories)

BENEFITS

Green Apple Glory is a sweet and earthy juice packed with vitamins K, C, and A, promoting bone health, a healthy immune system, and good vision.

ZESTY ZUCCHINI

Weight: 1.2 kg   Total Calorie Count: 414 Calories

INGREDIENTS

- 600g Zucchinis (102 calories)
- 600g Apples (312 calories)

BENEFITS

Zesty Zucchini is a sweet and refreshing juice. Zucchinis are a good source of vitamins C and B6, promoting a healthy immune system and good brain function. Apples add extra sweetness and vitamin C.

Juicing for beginners

LETTUCE LOVE

Weight: 1.1 kg   **Total Calorie Count: 398 Calories**

INGREDIENTS

- 600g Romaine Lettuce (106 calories)
- 500g Pears (292 calories)

BENEFITS

Lettuce Love is a sweet and crisp juice. Romaine lettuce is rich in vitamin K, promoting bone health. Pears add sweetness, fiber, and vitamin C.

PINEAPPLE PEPPER

Weight: 1.1 kg   **Total Calorie Count: 450 Calories**

INGREDIENTS

- 600g Pineapples (300 calories)
- 500g Bell Peppers (150 calories)

BENEFITS

Pineapple Pepper is a sweet, slightly spicy juice. Pineapples provide an excellent source of vitamin C and digestive benefits. Bell peppers add extra vitamin C and a slight kick.

Kara Kemp

FRUITY FENNEL

Weight: 1.2 kg   **Total Calorie Count: 480 Calories**

INGREDIENTS

- 600g Fennel (168 calories)
- 600g Apples (312 calories)

BENEFITS

Fruity Fennel is a sweet and slightly licorice-flavored juice. Fennel is rich in vitamin C and fiber, promoting a healthy immune system and aiding digestion. Apples add extra sweetness and vitamin C.

CHERRY CUCUMBER

Weight: 1.2 kg   **Total Calorie Count: 456 Calories**

INGREDIENTS

- 600g Cherries (360 calories)
- 600g Cucumbers (96 calories)

BENEFITS

Cherry Cucumber is a sweet and hydrating juice. Cherries are rich in antioxidants, promoting heart health. Cucumbers add hydration and vitamin K, promoting bone health.

Juicing for beginners

BLUEBERRY BEET

Weight: 1.2 kg   Total Calorie Count: 585 Calories

INGREDIENTS

- 600g Beetroots (252 calories)
- 600g Blueberries (333 calories)

BENEFITS

Blueberry Beet is a sweet, earthy juice, rich in antioxidants from blueberries and beneficial for heart health due to beetroots.

MANGO MELON

Weight: 1.3 kg   Total Calorie Count: 600 Calories

INGREDIENTS

- 700g Mangoes (420 calories)
- 600g Melons (180 calories)

BENEFITS

Mango Melon is a tropical, sweet juice. Mangoes and melons are rich in vitamins A and C, promoting skin health and a healthy immune system.

Kara Kemp

KIWI KALE

Weight: 1.1 kg   **Total Calorie Count: 526 Calories**

INGREDIENTS

- 600g Kiwis (276 calories)
- 500g Kale (250 calories)

BENEFITS

Kiwi Kale is a slightly tangy and earthy juice packed with vitamins K, C, and A from kale. Kiwis add extra vitamin C and a sweet tang.

PEAR PARSNIP

Weight: 1.2 kg   **Total Calorie Count: 770 Calories**

INGREDIENTS

- 600g Pears (350 calories)
- 600g Parsnips (420 calories)

BENEFITS

Pear Parsnip is a sweet, slightly spicy juice. Pears offer a good source of vitamin C and fiber, promoting a healthy immune system and aiding digestion. Parsnips add a good source of vitamin C and fiber.

Juicing for beginners

APRICOT ARTICHOKE

Weight: 1.2 kg **Total Calorie Count: 600 Calories**

INGREDIENTS

- 600g Apricots (300 calories)
- 600g Artichokes (300 calories)

BENEFITS

Apricot Artichoke is a sweet, slightly earthy juice. Apricots are rich in vitamins A and C, promoting skin health and a healthy immune system. Artichokes are a good source of fiber, aiding in digestion.

PINEAPPLE PARSLEY

Weight: 1.2 kg **Total Calorie Count: 625 Calories**

INGREDIENTS

- 700g Pineapples (350 calories)
- 500g Parsley (275 calories)

BENEFITS

Pineapple Parsley is a tropical, slightly spicy juice. Pineapples provide a good source of vitamin C and digestive benefits. Parsley is rich in vitamin K, promoting bone health.

Kara Kemp

CITRUS SPLASH

Weight: 1.2 kg   Total Calorie Count: 435 Calories

INGREDIENTS

- 300g Oranges (144 calories)
- 300g Grapefruits (120 calories)
- 300g Lemons (87 calories)
- 300g Limes (84 calories)

BENEFITS

Citrus Splash is a tangy juice packed with vitamin C from all the citrus fruits. It helps in boosting the immune system and is a good antioxidant, which can help reduce the risk of chronic diseases.

TROPICAL GREEN

Weight: 1.2 kg   Total Calorie Count: 549 Calories

INGREDIENTS

- 300g Pineapples (150 calories)
- 300g Mangoes (180 calories)
- 300g Spinach (69 calories)
- 300g Kale (150 calories)

BENEFITS

Tropical Green is a sweet, tropical juice with a hint of earthiness from spinach and kale. It's loaded with vitamins C, A, and K, promoting a healthy immune system, good vision, and strong bones.

Juicing for beginners

BERRY GOODNESS

Weight: 1.2 kg	Total Calorie Count: 555 Calories

INGREDIENTS

- 240g Blueberries (136 calories)
- 240g Raspberries (120 calories)
- 240g Strawberries (77 calories)
- 240g Blackberries (98 calories)
- 240g Apples (124 calories)

BENEFITS

Berry Goodness is a sweet, tangy juice packed with antioxidants from all the berries. This can help reduce the risk of chronic diseases, while apples add fiber to aid digestion.

GREEN FRESH

Weight: 1.2 kg	Total Calorie Count: 409 Calories

INGREDIENTS

- 240g Cucumbers (48 calories)
- 240g Green Apples (125 calories)
- 240g Spinach (69 calories)
- 240g Celery (30 calories)
- 240g Parsley (137 calories)

BENEFITS

Green Fresh is a refreshing juice packed with vitamins K, C, and A from all the green ingredients. It supports bone health, aids digestion, and promotes a healthy immune system.

Kara Kemp

SPICY SWEET

Weight: 1.2 kg   Total Calorie Count: 660 Calories

INGREDIENTS

- 300g Pineapples (150 calories)
- 300g Oranges (144 calories)
- 300g Carrots (126 calories)
- 300g Ginger Root (240 calories)

BENEFITS

Spicy Sweet is a sweet, slightly spicy juice packed with vitamins C, A, and the benefits of ginger which aids digestion and reduces inflammation. This juice is ideal for a quick pick-me-up.

Juicing for beginners

Part 4: Basic Recipes

DETOX JUICES

Detox juices are an excellent way to pack a lot of nutrients into your diet while giving your digestive system a chance to rest and rejuvenate. In contrast, it's important to remember that no juice can single-handedly "detox" your body; certain ingredients can support your body's natural detoxification process. The following recipes come with specific weight measurements and approximate calorie counts.

As always, remember these are approximations, and actual calorie counts can vary based on your produce's specific variety and ripeness.

GREEN CLEANSE

Weight: 1 kg   **Total Calorie Count: 282 Calories**

INGREDIENTS

- 500g Cucumbers (80 calories)
- 250g Celery (40 calories)
- 150g Parsley (82 calories)
- 100g Ginger Root (80 calories)

DETOX BENEFITS

This blend aids in digestion, hydration, and inflammation reduction, promoting overall wellness. Cucumbers and celery are hydrating and help flush out toxins. Parsley is rich in antioxidants and anti-inflammatory properties, while ginger, a well-known digestive aid, can help the body process and eliminate toxins effectively.

USAGE

For best detox results, drink one serving of this juice on an empty stomach in the morning. If necessary, a second serving can be consumed in the late afternoon.

CITRUS DETOX

Weight: 1 kg   **Total Calorie Count: 384 Calories**

INGREDIENTS

- 300g Oranges (144 calories)
- 300g Grapefruits (120 calories)
- 200g Lemons (60 calories)
- 200g Limes (60 calories)

DETOX BENEFITS

Berry Goodness is a sweet, tangy juice packed with antioxidants from all the berries. This can help reduce the risk of chronic diseases, while apples add fiber to aid digestion.

USAGE

Enjoy a glass of Citrus Detox first thing in the morning for a refreshing start to your day or as an afternoon pick-me-up.

BEET AND BERRY PURIFIER

Weight: 1.2 kg   **Total Calorie Count: 640 Calories**

INGREDIENTS

- 400g Beetroots (168 calories)
- 400g Blueberries (228 calories)
- 200g Carrots (84 calories)
- 200g Ginger Root (160 calories)

DETOX BENEFITS

Beetroots are known for their ability to help cleanse the liver, one of the body's primary detox organs. Blueberries are packed with antioxidants, aiding in neutralizing harmful free radicals. Carrots and ginger, meanwhile, help improve digestion.

USAGE

Start your day with a glass of Beet and Berry Purifier, or enjoy it as a mid-afternoon snack to stimulate detoxification.

Juicing for beginners

TROPICAL FLUSH

Weight: 1 kg   **Total Calorie Count: 570 Calories**

INGREDIENTS

- 400g Pineapples (200 calories)
- 300g Papaya (120 calories)
- 200g Ginger Root (160 calories)
- 100g Turmeric Root (90 calories)

DETOX BENEFITS

Pineapple and papaya are rich in enzymes that aid digestion, while ginger and turmeric provide additional anti-inflammatory benefits, helping the body to recover from toxic overload.

USAGE

Drinking a serving of Tropical Flush in the morning or after meals can aid digestion and promote detoxification.

GREEN GINGER ALE

Weight: 1 kg   **Total Calorie Count: 479 Calories**

INGREDIENTS

- 500g Green Apples (260 calories)
- 250g Spinach (69 calories)
- 150g Ginger Root (120 calories)
- 100g Lime (30 calories)

DETOX BENEFITS

This blend's apples and spinach offer an array of antioxidants and vitamins, while ginger helps to improve digestion and reduce inflammation, key for aiding the body in processing and eliminating toxins.

USAGE

A glass in the morning can kickstart your digestion for the day, and an afternoon serving can help maintain digestive health.

Kara Kemp

MORNING SUNSHINE DETOX

Weight: 1.2 kg   Total Calorie Count: 652 Calories

INGREDIENTS

- 500g Carrots (210 calories)
- 400g Oranges (192 calories)
- 200g Ginger Root (160 calories)
- 100g Turmeric Root (90 calories)

DETOX BENEFITS

Carrots are rich in beta-carotene and fiber, aiding digestion and detoxification. Oranges provide a burst of vitamin C, while ginger and turmeric have potent anti-inflammatory and antioxidant effects.

USAGE

A glass of Morning Sunshine Detox juice is a vibrant way to start your day, aiding digestion, detoxification, and immunity-boosting.

SWEET GREEN DETOX

Weight: 1 kg   Total Calorie Count: 392 Calories

INGREDIENTS

- 500g Green Apples (260 calories)
- 300g Cucumbers (60 calories)
- 100g Spinach (23 calories)
- 100g Parsley (49 calories)

DETOX BENEFITS

This blend combines antioxidant-rich apples with hydrating cucumbers and nutrient-dense greens for a refreshing detox juice.

USAGE

Ideal for an afternoon snack or a pre-meal appetizer to aid digestion and nutrient absorption.

Juicing for beginners

TROPICAL TURMERIC CLEANSE

Weight: 1 kg   Total Calorie Count: 528 Calories

INGREDIENTS

- 600g Pineapples (300 calories)
- 200g Oranges (96 calories)
- 100g Carrots (42 calories)
- 100g Turmeric Root (90 calories)

DETOX BENEFITS

This blend leverages the digestive enzyme bromelain from pineapple, the hydration and vitamin C from oranges, and the anti-inflammatory properties of turmeric.

USAGE

Best consumed in the morning to stimulate digestion and enhance hydration.

CUCUMBER MINT DETOX

Weight: 1 kg   Total Calorie Count: 292 Calories

INGREDIENTS

- 700g Cucumbers (140 calories)
- 200g Apples (104 calories)
- 100g Mint (48 calories)

DETOX BENEFITS

A hydrating and refreshing detox juice thanks to cucumber, with mint promoting digestion and apples, add a hint of sweetness and antioxidants.

USAGE

A refreshing drink to enjoy daily to support ongoing detoxification.

Kara Kemp

BEETROOT GINGER DETOX

Weight: 1 kg   **Total Calorie Count: 446 Calories**

INGREDIENTS

- 600g Beetroots (252 calories)
- 200g Carrots (84 calories)
- 100g Ginger Root (80 calories)
- 100g Lemon (30 calories)

DETOX BENEFITS

A potent detoxifier thanks to beetroot's ability to support liver function, with added benefits from ginger's digestive aid and lemon's vitamin C.

USAGE

Ideal for consumption in the morning or before meals to stimulate digestion and support liver function.

KALE LEMONADE DETOX

Weight: 1 kg   **Total Calorie Count: 451 Calories**

INGREDIENTS

- 500g Kale (245 calories)
- 300g Apples (156 calories)
- 100g Cucumbers (20 calories)
- 100g Lemon (30 calories)

DETOX BENEFITS

Kale's dense nutrient profile and high fiber content aid detoxification, while apples, cucumber, and lemon add hydration and vitamin C.

USAGE

Best consumed in the morning or midday for nutrient-rich hydration and detoxification support.

Juicing for beginners

CELERY AND APPLE FLUSH

Weight: 1 kg   Total Calorie Count: 347 Calories

INGREDIENTS

- 500g Green Apples (260 calories)
- 400g Celery (64 calories)
- 100g Spinach (23 calories)

DETOX BENEFITS

This blend offers a refreshing mix of hydration and fiber, assisting in regular bowel movements, an essential part of the detox process.

USAGE

Best consumed in the morning to stimulate digestion and flush toxins.

PEAR GINGER CLEANSE

Weight: 1 kg   Total Calorie Count: 617 Calories

INGREDIENTS

- 500g Pears (267 calories)
- 400g Ginger Root (320 calories)
- 100g Lemon (30 calories)

DETOX BENEFITS

Pears and ginger promote healthy digestion, while lemon adds vitamin C and aids in alkalizing the body.

USAGE

Drink in the morning or as an afternoon refresher to aid digestion and detox.

Kara Kemp

PINEAPPLE BEET DETOX

Weight: 1 kg   **Total Calorie Count: 414 Calories**

INGREDIENTS

- 400g Pineapples (200 calories)
- 300g Beetroots (126 calories)
- 200g Cucumber (40 calories)
- 100g Mint (48 calories)

DETOX BENEFITS

Pineapple's bromelain helps digestion, beetroot supports liver function, and cucumber hydrates while mint freshens the taste and soothes the stomach.

USAGE

Drink in the morning or after meals to support digestive and liver health.

CANTALOUPE & GINGER BLEND

Weight: 1 kg   **Total Calorie Count: 424 Calories**

INGREDIENTS

- 600g Cantaloupes (180 calories)
- 200g Ginger Root (160 calories)
- 200g Carrots (84 calories)

DETOX BENEFITS

Cantaloupes are hydrating, ginger aids digestion, and carrots provide beneficial antioxidants and fiber.

USAGE

Ideal for an afternoon snack to aid digestion and keep you hydrated.

Juicing for beginners

WATERMELON AND MINT COOLER

Weight: 1 kg   Total Calorie Count: 298 Calories

INGREDIENTS

- 700g Watermelon (210 calories)
- 200g Cucumbers (40 calories)
- 100g Mint (48 calories)

DETOX BENEFITS

This blend is exceptionally hydrating and refreshing, helping your body flush out toxins.

USAGE

A great juice to enjoy throughout a hot day to maintain hydration and gently detoxify.

SPICY LEMON DETOX

Weight: 1 kg   Total Calorie Count: 420 Calories

INGREDIENTS

- 400g Lemons (120 calories)
- 300g Ginger Root (240 calories)
- 300g Cucumber (60 calories)

DETOX BENEFITS

Lemons are rich in Vitamin C and promote alkalinity, ginger aids digestion, and cucumber offers hydration.

USAGE

Perfect as a morning juice to stimulate digestion and boost immune health.

Kara Kemp

TANGY CRANBERRY DETOX

Weight: 1 kg   **Total Calorie Count: 491 Calories**

INGREDIENTS

- 700g Cranberries (315 calories)
- 200g Oranges (96 calories)
- 100g Ginger Root (80 calories)

DETOX BENEFITS

Cranberries are excellent for urinary health, oranges provide vitamin C, and ginger aids digestion.

USAGE

Drink in the morning or anytime daily to support urinary health and detoxification.

POMEGRANATE AND BERRY CLEANSE

Weight: 1 kg   **Total Calorie Count: 602 Calories**

INGREDIENTS

- 500g Pomegranates (332 calories)
- 300g Raspberries (156 calories)
- 200g Blueberries (114 calories)

DETOX BENEFITS

This blend is a powerhouse of antioxidants from berries and pomegranates, aiding in neutralizing harmful free radicals.

USAGE

Best consumed in the morning or midday for nutrient-rich hydration and detoxification support.

Juicing for beginners

COOL CUCUMBER CLEANSE

Weight: 1 kg   **Total Calorie Count: 256 Calories**

INGREDIENTS

- 800g Cucumbers (160 calories)
- 200g Mint (96 calories)

DETOX BENEFITS

Cucumbers are hydrating and beneficial for skin health, while mint promotes digestion.

USAGE

Enjoy throughout the day for hydration and digestive health.

VIBRANT CARROT & GINGER

Weight: 1 kg   **Total Calorie Count: 516 Calories**

INGREDIENTS

- 600g Carrots (252 calories)
- 200g Apples (104 calories)
- 200g Ginger Root (160 calories)

DETOX BENEFITS

Carrots provide vitamin A, which benefits the immune system and vision, while ginger aids digestion. Apples add sweetness and are high in fiber and vitamin C.

USAGE

Ideal for an afternoon snack or a pre-meal appetizer to aid digestion and nutrient absorption.

Kara Kemp

SWEET PINEAPPLE GREENS

Weight: 1 kg   **Total Calorie Count: 473 Calories**

INGREDIENTS

- 400g Pineapples (200 calories)
- 300g Kale (147 calories)
- 200g Spinach (46 calories)
- 100g Ginger Root (80 calories)

DETOX BENEFITS

Pineapples aid digestion, while kale and spinach provide abundant nutrients. Ginger acts as an excellent digestive aid and offers anti-inflammatory benefits.

USAGE

Perfect for a morning boost or as an afternoon snack.

BERRY BLAST DETOX

Weight: 1 kg   **Total Calorie Count: 463 Calories**

INGREDIENTS

- 300g Strawberries (96 calories)
- 300g Blueberries (171 calories)
- 200g Raspberries (104 calories)
- 200g Blackberries (92 calories)

DETOX BENEFITS

Berries are loaded with antioxidants, which can help your body fight inflammation and protect cells from damage.

USAGE

Enjoy this juice in the morning or throughout the day for a nutrient-dense, antioxidant-rich refreshment.

Juicing for beginners

GINGER SPICE DETOX

Weight: 1 kg   **Total Calorie Count: 556 Calories**

INGREDIENTS

- 500g Apples (260 calories)
- 300g Carrots (126 calories)
- 100g Ginger Root (80 calories)
- 100g Turmeric Root (90 calories)

DETOX BENEFITS

Apples and carrots provide essential nutrients, while ginger and turmeric have potent anti-inflammatory and antioxidant effects.

USAGE

Best consumed in the morning or midday for nutrient-rich hydration and detoxification support.

.

Kara Kemp

Part 4: Basic Recipes

ENERGY-BOOSTING JUICES

Feeling a midday slump or need a pre-workout boost? An energy-boosting juice can be a healthy and refreshing solution. These nutrient-dense juices are full of vitamins and antioxidants that can enhance your energy levels and keep you going throughout the day. Each recipe includes specific weight measurements for each ingredient and the approximate calorie count.

Please keep in mind that these calorie counts are approximate and may vary slightly depending on your produce's specific variety and ripeness.

CITRUS SUNRISE

Weight: 1 kg   Total Calorie Count: 456 Calories

INGREDIENTS

- 400g Oranges (192 calories)
- 300g Grapefruits (144 calories)
- 300g Lemons (120 calories)

ENERGY BOOSTING BENEFITS

Citrus fruits like oranges, grapefruits, and lemons are rich in vitamin C, which helps enhance immunity and energy levels.

USAGE

Enjoy this juice in the morning for an energetic start to your day.

APPLE BERRY BLISS

Weight: 1 kg   **Total Calorie Count: 470 Calories**

INGREDIENTS

- 500g Apples (260 calories)
- 300g Strawberries (96 calories)
- 200g Blueberries (114 calories)

ENERGY BOOSTING BENEFITS

The natural sugars in apples, strawberries, and blueberries provide quick energy while the fiber keeps your energy steady.

USAGE

Great for a midday pick-me-up or post-workout recovery juice.

CARROT GINGER ZING

Weight: 1 kg   **Total Calorie Count: 488 Calories**

INGREDIENTS

- 600g Carrots (252 calories)
- 300g Apples (156 calories)
- 100g Ginger Root (80 calories)

ENERGY BOOSTING BENEFITS

Carrots provide a quick energy source due to their natural sugars, while ginger stimulates blood circulation.

USAGE

This juice is perfect for an afternoon energy boost.

Kara Kemp

TROPICAL ENERGIZER

Weight: 1 kg   **Total Calorie Count: 532 Calories**

INGREDIENTS

- 500g Pineapples (250 calories)
- 300g Mangoes (186 calories)
- 200g Oranges (96 calories)

ENERGY BOOSTING BENEFITS

Pineapples, mangoes, and oranges are rich in vitamins and minerals that can boost your energy levels and improve physical performance.

USAGE

Enjoy this juice as a morning treat or an afternoon energy booster.

KALE POWER PUNCH

Weight: 1 kg   **Total Calorie Count: 450 Calories**

INGREDIENTS

- 500g Kale (245 calories)
- 250g Apples (130 calories)
- 250g Lemons (75 calories)

ENERGY BOOSTING BENEFITS

Kale is a nutrient-dense food packed with vitamins and minerals that can improve energy levels, while apples and lemons provide quick energy due to their natural sugars.

USAGE

Ideal for a pre-workout boost or a refreshing pick-me-up anytime during the day.

SWEET BEET RUSH

Weight: 1 kg   **Total Calorie Count: 460 Calories**

INGREDIENTS

- 500g Beets (220 calories)
- 300g Apples (156 calories)
- 200g Carrots (84 calories)

ENERGY BOOSTING BENEFITS

Beets contain nitrates that improve blood flow, increasing stamina and energy levels.

USAGE

Perfect before a workout to improve performance.

PINEAPPLE GINGER ZEST

Weight: 1 kg   **Total Calorie Count: 524 Calories**

INGREDIENTS

- 600g Pineapples (300 calories)
- 300g Oranges (144 calories)
- 100g Ginger Root (80 calories)

ENERGY BOOSTING BENEFITS

Pineapples and oranges provide quick energy and vitamin C, while ginger stimulates blood flow.

USAGE

Excellent as a morning energy booster or post-workout recovery drink.

Kara Kemp

GREEN ENERGY MACHINE

Weight: 1 kg   Total Calorie Count: 296 Calories

INGREDIENTS

- 400g Spinach (92 calories)
- 300g Apples (156 calories)
- 200g Cucumbers (32 calories)
- 100g Celery (16 calories)

ENERGY BOOSTING BENEFITS

The iron in spinach helps with energy production, and the hydration from cucumbers and celery helps with overall energy balance.

USAGE

Ideal for mid-morning or afternoon slumps.

TROPICAL GREEN RUSH

Weight: 1 kg   Total Calorie Count: 452 Calories

INGREDIENTS

- 400g Pineapples (200 calories)
- 300g Spinach (69 calories)
- 300g Kiwis (183 calories)

ENERGY BOOSTING BENEFITS

Kiwis and pineapples are high in vitamins C and E, providing energy and antioxidants, while spinach offers iron for energy production.

USAGE

Great as a morning start or afternoon pick-me-up.

Juicing for beginners

SWEET MELON BURST

Weight: 1 kg | **Total Calorie Count: 340 Calories**

INGREDIENTS

- 600g Watermelon (180 calories)
- 200g Cantaloupe (68 calories)
- 200g Honeydew Melon (92 calories)

ENERGY BOOSTING BENEFITS

Melons are rich in electrolytes and water, making them excellent for energy and hydration.

USAGE

Best enjoyed on hot days for a refreshing, energy-boosting treat.

ZESTY LEMON LIFT

Weight: 1 kg | **Total Calorie Count: 480 Calories**

INGREDIENTS

- 500g Lemons (150 calories)
- 250g Apples (130 calories)
- 250g Ginger Root (200 calories)

ENERGY BOOSTING BENEFITS

Lemons and apples provide quick, natural sugar energy, and ginger stimulates blood flow, increasing power.

USAGE

Perfect for a morning boost or an afternoon lift.

Kara Kemp

RASPBERRY REVITALIZER

Weight: 1 kg　　　　**Total Calorie Count: 512 Calories**

INGREDIENTS

- 500g Raspberries (260 calories)
- 300g Apples (156 calories)
- 200g Oranges (96 calories)

ENERGY BOOSTING BENEFITS

Raspberries are high in fiber, maintaining stable blood sugar levels for consistent energy. Apples and oranges provide immediate power.

USAGE

Ideal as a mid-morning snack or pre-workout energy source.

VIBRANT VEGGIE VITALITY

Weight: 1 kg　　　　**Total Calorie Count: 244 Calories**

INGREDIENTS

- 300g Carrots (126 calories)
- 300g Tomatoes (54 calories)
- 200g Cucumbers (32 calories)
- 200g Celery (32 calories)

ENERGY BOOSTING BENEFITS

Carrots and tomatoes offer energy-producing nutrients, while cucumber and celery hydrate, aiding overall energy balance.

USAGE

An excellent midday pick-me-up, providing sustained energy without a sugar crash.

Juicing for beginners

CITRUS CARROT BLAST

Weight: 1 kg | **Total Calorie Count: 405 Calories**

INGREDIENTS

- 500g Carrots (210 calories)
- 250g Oranges (120 calories)
- 250g Lemons (75 calories)

ENERGY BOOSTING BENEFITS

Carrots provide quick energy, while citrus fruits are high in vitamin C, boosting immunity and energy.

USAGE

Enjoy this juice in the morning for a lively start to your day.

STRAWBERRY KIWI KICKSTART

Weight: 1 kg | **Total Calorie Count: 451 Calories**

INGREDIENTS

- 500g Strawberries (160 calories)
- 500g Kiwis (291 calories)

ENERGY BOOSTING BENEFITS

Both strawberries and kiwis are high in vitamin C and provide a natural energy boost.

USAGE

Perfect as a mid-morning snack or pre-workout juice.

Kara Kemp

CUCUMBER COOLER

Weight: 1 kg   **Total Calorie Count: 202 Calories**

INGREDIENTS

- 700g Cucumbers (112 calories)
- 300g Lemons (90 calories)

ENERGY BOOSTING BENEFITS

Cucumbers are excellent hydrated and rich in B vitamins, helping sustain energy levels. Lemons add a zesty flavor and additional vitamin C.

USAGE

Ideal for a refreshing, energy-sustaining afternoon drink.

POWERHOUSE PEAR & SPINACH

Weight: 1 kg   **Total Calorie Count: 403 Calories**

INGREDIENTS

- 500g Pears (302 calories)
- 300g Spinach (69 calories)
- 200g Cucumbers (32 calories)

ENERGY BOOSTING BENEFITS

Pears offer a quick energy boost due to their high natural sugar content, while spinach provides iron for energy production.

USAGE

Perfect for an afternoon energy lift.

Juicing for beginners

PINEAPPLE MINT REFRESH

Weight: 1 kg   Total Calorie Count: 488 Calories

INGREDIENTS

- 800g Pineapples (400 calories)
- 200g Mint Leaves (88 calories)

ENERGY BOOSTING BENEFITS

Pineapples provide quick energy and hydrating electrolytes, while mint stimulates digestion and enhances mood.

USAGE

Enjoy this refreshing juice as a morning energy boost or mid-afternoon pick-me-up.

CELERY CITRUS ENERGIZER

Weight: 1 kg   Total Calorie Count: 296 Calories

INGREDIENTS

- 500g Celery (80 calories)
- 250g Oranges (120 calories)
- 250g Grapefruits (96 calories)

ENERGY BOOSTING BENEFITS

Celery is hydrating and low in sugar, providing steady energy, while citrus fruits offer quick points.

USAGE

Ideal for a low-calorie, energy-sustaining morning or afternoon drink.

Kara Kemp

APPLE AVOCADO DELIGHT

Weight: 1 kg

Total Calorie Count: 1060 Calories

INGREDIENTS

- 500g Apples (260 calories)
- 500g Avocados (800 calories)

ENERGY BOOSTING BENEFITS

Apples provide immediate energy from natural sugars, while avocados offer healthy fats and fiber for sustained energy.

USAGE

This higher-calorie juice is perfect for a meal replacement or a substantial energy boost.

Juicing for beginners

Part 4: Basic Recipes

IMMUNE-BOOSTING JUICES

In a world where health is a primary concern, immune-boosting juices are gaining popularity for their potential to provide essential vitamins and antioxidants that support the immune system. Here are a few delicious and nutritious juice recipes designed to boost your immune system. Each recipe includes specific weight measurements and an estimated calorie count.

Remember that the following calorie counts are approximate and can vary based on your produce's specific variety and ripeness.

CHERRY CINNAMON CHARM

Weight: 1 kg   Total Calorie Count: 841 Calories

INGREDIENTS

- 700g Cherries (490 calories)
- 200g Apples (104 calories)
- 100g Cinnamon (247 calories)

IMMUNE-BOOSTING BENEFITS

·Cherries are packed with antioxidants and anti-inflammatory compounds.
·Apples provide dietary fiber and vitamin C.
·Cinnamon adds a sweet spice and has anti-inflammatory properties.

USAGE
Ideal as a dessert juice or a sweet treat during the day.

Kara Kemp

PARSLEY PEPPER PUNCH

Weight: 1 kg   Total Calorie Count: 647 Calories

INGREDIENTS

- 600g Parsley (216 calories)
- 200g Tomatoes (36 calories)
- 100g Green Pepper (20 calories)
- 100g Cumin (375 calories)

IMMUNE-BOOSTING BENEFITS

Parsley is rich in vitamin K and vitamin C and has anti-inflammatory properties; tomatoes and green pepper are high in antioxidants, and cumin adds a spicy kick and can aid digestion.

USAGE

A refreshing juice to kickstart your morning or as a mid-afternoon snack.

CITRUS GINGER GLORY

Weight: 1 kg   Total Calorie Count: 544 Calories

INGREDIENTS

- 500g Oranges (240 calories)
- 300g Grapefruit (144 calories)
- 200g Ginger (160 calories)

IMMUNE-BOOSTING BENEFITS

Oranges and grapefruit provide a high dose of vitamin C, and ginger offers anti-inflammatory and antioxidant effects.

USAGE

Ideal as a morning or post-workout drink.

Juicing for beginners

GREEN GARLIC GUSTO

Weight: 1 kg   **Total Calorie Count: 511 Calories**

INGREDIENTS

- 700g Spinach (161 calories)
- 200g Garlic (320 calories)
- 100g Lime (30 calories)

IMMUNE-BOOSTING BENEFITS

·Spinach is rich in iron and vitamin C.
·Garlic has strong antibacterial properties.
·Lime adds a tart flavor and more vitamin C.

USAGE

A savory juice perfect for lunch or an afternoon pick-me-up.

RADISH ROSEMARY RUSH

Weight: 1 kg   **Total Calorie Count: 301 Calories**

INGREDIENTS

- 600g Radishes (108 calories)
- 200g Celery (32 calories)
- 100g Rosemary (131 calories)
- 100g Lemons (30 calories)

IMMUNE-BOOSTING BENEFITS

Radishes and celery offer vitamin C and other nutrients; Rosemary adds a unique flavor and has anti-inflammatory properties. Lemons enhance the immune-boosting potential with more vitamin C.

USAGE

A uniquely flavored juice, perfect for those seeking something different.

Kara Kemp

SPICED CARROT KICK

Weight: 1 kg   Total Calorie Count: 476 Calories

INGREDIENTS

- 600g Carrots (252 calories)
- 300g Oranges (144 calories)
- 100g Ginger (80 calories)

IMMUNE-BOOSTING BENEFITS

·Carrots are rich in vitamin A.
·Oranges offer a vitamin C boost.
·Ginger adds a zesty taste and anti-inflammatory benefits.

USAGE

Ideal as a morning juice to start your day with energy.

PEPPERED PINEAPPLE DELIGHT

Weight: 1 kg   Total Calorie Count: 468 Calories

INGREDIENTS

- 800g Pineapple (400 calories)
- 200g Cayenne Pepper (68 calories)

IMMUNE-BOOSTING BENEFITS

Pineapple is packed with bromelain that aids digestion and has anti-inflammatory properties, while cayenne pepper is known to boost metabolism.

USAGE

This spicy sweet juice is excellent as a post-meal digestive aid.

TURMERIC BEET BLAST

Weight: 1 kg   **Total Calorie Count: 678 Calories**

INGREDIENTS

- 500g Beets (210 calories)
- 300g Apples (156 calories)
- 200g Turmeric (312 calories)

IMMUNE-BOOSTING BENEFITS

Beets are packed with essential nutrients, apples add sweetness and antioxidants, and turmeric provides powerful anti-inflammatory benefits.

USAGE

A great afternoon pick-me-up to keep your energy high.

GINGER GREENS

Weight: 1 kg   **Total Calorie Count: 345 Calories**

INGREDIENTS

- 500g Kale (205 calories)
- 400g Cucumber (60 calories)
- 100g Ginger (80 calories)

IMMUNE-BOOSTING BENEFITS

Kale provides vitamins K, A, and C, cucumber hydrates, and ginger adds a spicy kick with anti-inflammatory properties.

USAGE

Perfect for a post-workout drink to replenish your body.

Kara Kemp

SPICED CITRUS SURPRISE

Weight: 1 kg   Total Calorie Count: 625 Calories

INGREDIENTS

- 600g Oranges (288 calories)
- 300g Lemon (90 calories)
- 100g Cinnamon (247 calories)

IMMUNE-BOOSTING BENEFITS

Oranges and lemons provide a high amount of vitamin C, while cinnamon adds a warming flavor and can reduce inflammation.

USAGE

A delicious juice for breakfast or an afternoon snack.

CELERY CUMIN COOLER

Weight: 1 kg   Total Calorie Count: 969 Calories

INGREDIENTS

- 800g Celery (112 calories)
- 200g Cumin (857 calories)

IMMUNE-BOOSTING BENEFITS

Celery provides a wealth of antioxidants, while cumin offers a distinctive flavor and is known for its potential immune-boosting properties.

USAGE

Perfect as a refreshing and unique twist to a midday juice.

Juicing for beginners

PEPPERMINT PAPAYA PUNCH

Weight: 1 kg   Total Calorie Count: 432 Calories

INGREDIENTS

- 800g Papaya (336 calories)
- 200g Peppermint (96 calories)

IMMUNE-BOOSTING BENEFITS

Papaya is rich in vitamin C, fiber, and antioxidants, while peppermint adds a refreshing twist and aids digestion.

USAGE

Perfect as a dessert drink or to soothe a sensitive stomach.

TOMATO TURMERIC TONIC

Weight: 1 kg   Total Calorie Count: 456 Calories

INGREDIENTS

- 800g Tomatoes (144 calories)
- 200g Turmeric (312 calories)

IMMUNE-BOOSTING BENEFITS

Tomatoes are packed with lycopene, a powerful antioxidant, and turmeric offers anti-inflammatory benefits.

USAGE

A savory juice perfect for lunch or dinner.

Kara Kemp

GARLIC GREENS

Weight: 1 kg **Total Calorie Count: 504 Calories**

INGREDIENTS

- 800g Spinach (184 calories)
- 200g Garlic (320 calories)

IMMUNE-BOOSTING BENEFITS

Spinach provides a variety of vitamins and minerals, while garlic boosts the immune system and can fight infection.

USAGE

An interesting savory juice for an adventurous palate.

ZESTY ZUCCHINI ZEN

Weight: 1 kg **Total Calorie Count: 246 Calories**

INGREDIENTS

- 800g Zucchini (136 calories)
- 100g Lemon (30 calories)
- 100g Ginger (80 calories)

IMMUNE-BOOSTING BENEFITS

Zucchini is a good source of health-protecting antioxidants and vitamin C, while ginger and lemon add a flavorful zest and additional immune support.

USAGE

Ideal for an evening cleanse or a pre-bedtime drink.

Juicing for beginners

KALE KICK

Weight: 1 kg   **Total Calorie Count: 490 Calories**

INGREDIENTS

- 600g Kale (246 calories)
- 400g Kiwi (244 calories)

IMMUNE-BOOSTING BENEFITS

Kale is rich in vitamin C and antioxidants, whereas kiwi offers a blast of vitamins C, K, and E, all beneficial for a robust immune system.

USAGE

Ideal as a breakfast juice to start your day with a vitamin-packed punch.

SWEET POTATO SURPRISE

Weight: 1 kg   **Total Calorie Count: 634 Calories**

INGREDIENTS

- 500g Sweet Potatoes (390 calories)
- 300g Oranges (144 calories)
- 200g Pineapple (100 calories)

IMMUNE-BOOSTING BENEFITS

Sweet potatoes are rich in beta carotene, which our body converts into vitamin A, crucial for a healthy immune system. Pineapples and oranges add a dash of vitamin C.

USAGE

Great as a mid-morning or mid-afternoon snack.

Kara Kemp

BROCCOLI BLAST

Weight: 1 kg   **Total Calorie Count: 401 Calories**

INGREDIENTS

- 700g Broccoli (245 calories)
- 300g Apples (156 calories)

IMMUNE-BOOSTING BENEFITS

Broccoli is power-packed with vitamins C, A, E, and fiber, while apples provide a sweet taste and additional antioxidants.

USAGE

Perfect for lunch or an afternoon boost.

PEPPERED PEAR

Weight: 1 kg   **Total Calorie Count: 516 Calories**

INGREDIENTS

- 600g Pears (360 calories)
- 200g Red Bell Peppers (60 calories)
- 200g Oranges (96 calories)

IMMUNE-BOOSTING BENEFITS

Pears and oranges provide vitamin C and fiber, while red bell peppers are incredibly high in vitamin C, making this a potent immune-boosting drink.

USAGE

This juice can be consumed anytime during the day.

Juicing for beginners

MELON MINT

Weight: 1 kg   **Total Calorie Count: 288 Calories**

INGREDIENTS

- 800g Watermelon (240 calories)
- 200g Mint Leaves (48 calories)

IMMUNE-BOOSTING BENEFITS

Watermelon is high in vitamins A and C, while mint adds a refreshing taste and additional antioxidants.

USAGE

A hydrating drink perfect for warm days or post-workout refreshments.

CITRUS SUNSHINE

Weight: 1 kg   **Total Calorie Count: 378 Calories**

INGREDIENTS

- 300g Oranges (144 calories)
- 300g Grapefruits (114 calories)
- 400g Lemons (120 calories)

IMMUNE-BOOSTING BENEFITS

Citrus fruits like oranges, grapefruits, and lemons are rich in vitamin C, known for boosting the immune system.

USAGE

This juice can be consumed in the morning to kickstart the day.

Kara Kemp

TURMERIC TANG

Weight: 1 kg   **Total Calorie Count: 752 Calories**

INGREDIENTS

- 500g Oranges (240 calories)
- 250g Ginger Root (200 calories)
- 250g Turmeric Root (312 calories)

IMMUNE-BOOSTING BENEFITS

Turmeric and ginger both have potent anti-inflammatory and antioxidant benefits, which aid in boosting the immune system.

USAGE

Consume it during the day to give your immune system a boost.

GREEN DEFENDER

Weight: 1 kg   **Total Calorie Count: 431 Calories**

INGREDIENTS

- 500g Spinach (115 calories)
- 300g Apples (156 calories)
- 200g Ginger Root (160 calories)

IMMUNE-BOOSTING BENEFITS

Spinach is rich in vitamin C, numerous antioxidants, and beta carotene, which can increase the infection-fighting ability of our immune system.

USAGE

This juice can be consumed anytime during the day.

Juicing for beginners

BERRY BLISS

Weight: 1 kg   **Total Calorie Count: 435 Calories**

INGREDIENTS

- 500g Strawberries (160 calories)
- 250g Blueberries (145 calories)
- 250g Raspberries (130 calories)

IMMUNE-BOOSTING BENEFITS

Berries are packed with antioxidants like anthocyanins, which protect the immune system from damage.

USAGE

This juice is perfect for a midday snack or a dessert drink.

VITAMIN POWER PUNCH

Weight: 1 kg   **Total Calorie Count: 454 Calories**

INGREDIENTS

- 500g Carrots (210 calories)
- 300g Oranges (144 calories)
- 200g Pineapples (100 calories)

IMMUNE-BOOSTING BENEFITS

Carrots, oranges, and pineapples are high in vitamins and antioxidants that help support the immune system.

USAGE

This juice can be consumed at any time during the day.

Kara Kemp

Part 4: Basic Recipes

WELLNESS SHOTS

Wellness shots are small but mighty additions to any juicing routine. These concentrated doses of fruits, vegetables, and spices are designed to deliver maximum health benefits in a few sips. Below are some wellness shot recipes, including the weight of ingredients and estimated calorie counts.

As always, remember these are approximations, and actual calorie counts can vary based on your produce's specific variety and ripeness.

GINGER LEMON SHOT

Weight: 100g   Total Calorie Count: 65 Calories

INGREDIENTS

- 70g Ginger (56 calories)
- 30g Lemon (9 calories)

WELLNESS BENEFITS

Ginger is anti-inflammatory, while lemon is rich in Vitamin C. This shot can help boost your immune system and aid digestion.

TURMERIC BLAST SHOT

Weight: 100g   Total Calorie Count: 227 Calories

INGREDIENTS

- 70g Turmeric (218 calories)
- 30g Lemon (9 calories)

WELLNESS BENEFITS

Turmeric contains curcumin, a powerful anti-inflammatory compound, while lemon adds Vitamin C. This shot can help reduce inflammation in the body.

GREEN ENERGY SHOT

Weight: 100g   Total Calorie Count: 46 Calories

INGREDIENTS

- 50g Wheatgrass (21 calories)
- 50g Kale (25 calories)

WELLNESS BENEFITS

This shot combines wheatgrass and kale for a powerful boost of vitamins A, C, E, and K.

ANTIOXIDANT SHOT

Weight: 100g   Total Calorie Count: 109 Calories

INGREDIENTS

- 50g Acai Berries (70 calories)
- 50g Pomegranate (39 calories)

WELLNESS BENEFITS

Acai berries and pomegranate are both rich in antioxidants, which can help protect the body from damage by harmful molecules called free radicals.

Kara Kemp

BEET BOOST SHOT

Weight: 100g   **Total Calorie Count: 56 Calories**

INGREDIENTS

- 70g Beetroot (32 calories)
- 30g Ginger (24 calories)

WELLNESS BENEFITS

Beetroot helps lower blood pressure and boost stamina, while ginger is anti-inflammatory.

VITAMIN C SHOT

Weight: 100g   **Total Calorie Count: 44 Calories**

INGREDIENTS

- 70g Orange (35 calories)
- 30g Acerola Cherries (9 calories)

WELLNESS BENEFITS

This shot contains Vitamin C from oranges and acerola cherries, which can boost your immune system and skin health.

LIVER DETOX SHOT

Weight: 100g   **Total Calorie Count: 34 Calories**

INGREDIENTS

- 70g Milk Thistle (25 calories)
- 30g Lemon (9 calories)

WELLNESS BENEFITS

Milk thistle is known to support liver health, while lemon adds a dose of Vitamin C.

FAT BURNER SHOT

Weight: 100g	Total Calorie Count: 47 Calories

INGREDIENTS

- 70g Grapefruit (30 calories)
- 30g Cayenne Pepper (17 calories)

WELLNESS BENEFITS

Grapefruit helps improve insulin resistance and aids in weight loss, while cayenne pepper boosts metabolism.

DIGESTIVE AID SHOT

Weight: 100g	Total Calorie Count: 26 Calories

INGREDIENTS

- 70g Fennel (20 calories)
- 30g Mint (6 calories)

WELLNESS BENEFITS

Fennel and mint both aid in digestion and help soothe stomach discomfort.

BRAIN BOOSTER SHOT

Weight: 100g	Total Calorie Count: 101 Calories

INGREDIENTS

- 70g Blueberries (39 calories)
- 30g Walnuts (62 calories)

WELLNESS BENEFITS

Blueberries and walnuts are rich in antioxidants and beneficial plant compounds, supporting brain health and memory.

Kara Kemp

TURMERIC TONIC SHOT

Weight: 100g   **Total Calorie Count: 89 Calories**

INGREDIENTS

- 70g Turmeric (80 calories)
- 30g Lemon (9 calories)

WELLNESS BENEFITS

Turmeric contains curcumin, a potent anti-inflammatory and antioxidant. Lemon adds a dose of Vitamin C.

BEETROOT BLAST SHOT

Weight: 100g   **Total Calorie Count: 53 Calories**

INGREDIENTS

- 70g Beetroot (29 calories)
- 30g Ginger (24 calories)

WELLNESS BENEFITS

Beetroot is packed with vitamins and minerals and can help lower blood pressure. Ginger adds a kick and aids digestion.

CUCUMBER CALM SHOT

Weight: 100g   **Total Calorie Count: 17 Calories**

INGREDIENTS

- 70g Cucumber (8 calories)
- 30g Lemon (9 calories)

WELLNESS BENEFITS

Cucumber is hydrating and packed with vitamins and minerals. Lemon gives a vitamin C boost.

PAPAYA POWER SHOT

Weight: 100g   Total Calorie Count: 39 Calories

INGREDIENTS

- 70g Papaya (30 calories)
- 30g Lemon (9 calories)

WELLNESS BENEFITS

Papaya contains an enzyme called papain, known for aiding digestion. Lemon adds a vitamin C boost.

GREEN MACHINE SHOT

Weight: 100g   Total Calorie Count: 37 Calories

INGREDIENTS

- 50g Spinach (12 calories)
- 50g Kale (25 calories)

WELLNESS BENEFITS

Spinach and Kale are both nutrient-dense foods loaded with antioxidants.

LEMONGRASS LIFT SHOT

Weight: 100g   Total Calorie Count: 79 Calories

INGREDIENTS

- 70g Lemongrass (70 calories)
- 30g Lemon (9 calories)

WELLNESS BENEFITS

Lemongrass promotes healthy digestion and boosts red blood cell levels. Lemon adds a Vitamin C boost.

PUMPKIN POWER SHOT

Weight: 100g   **Total Calorie Count: 52 Calories**

INGREDIENTS

- 70g Pumpkin (28 calories)
- 30g Ginger (24 calories)

WELLNESS BENEFITS

Pumpkin is high in vitamin A and antioxidants, promoting eye health. Ginger aids digestion.

TANGY TOMATO SHOT

Weight: 100g   **Total Calorie Count: 21 Calories**

INGREDIENTS

- 70g Tomato (12 calories)
- 30g Lemon (9 calories)

WELLNESS BENEFITS

Tomato is a good source of vitamins A, C, K, and potassium. Lemon adds a vitamin C boost.

GINGER ZINGER SHOT

Weight: 100g   **Total Calorie Count: 65 Calories**

INGREDIENTS

- 70g Ginger (56 calories)
- 30g Lemon (9 calories)

WELLNESS BENEFITS

Ginger is known for its anti-nausea and anti-inflammatory properties. Lemon adds a vitamin C boost.

CHERRY CHEER SHOT

Weight: 100g　　　　Total Calorie Count: 55 Calories

INGREDIENTS

- 70g Tart Cherries (46 calories)
- 30g Lemon (9 calories)

WELLNESS BENEFITS

Tart cherries are packed with antioxidants.

MANGO MAGIC SHOT

Weight: 100g

Total Calorie Count: 55 Calories

INGREDIENTS

- 70g Mango (46 calories)
- 30g Lemon (9 calories)

WELLNESS BENEFITS

Mango is high in vitamin C and promotes digestive health. Lemon adds additional vitamin C.

BLACKBERRY BURST SHOT

Weight: 100g

Total Calorie Count: 40 Calories

INGREDIENTS

- 70g Blackberries (31 calories)
- 30g Lemon (9 calories)

WELLNESS BENEFITS

Blackberries are packed with antioxidants and vitamin C. Lemon adds vitamin C boost.

Kara Kemp

Part 5: Understanding Ratios and Creating Your Recipes

When it comes to making juice, ratios are essential. Percentages refer to the proportion of each ingredient you're using. For example, a 1:1 ratio would mean using equal amounts of both if you're creating juice with apples and carrots.

But why are these ratios important? Because they help to balance taste, sugar content, and nutrient diversity. A juice with too much fruit may taste great, but it could also contain high sugar levels. A fluid with too many leafy greens might be packed with nutrients, but its taste might be overwhelming, especially for juicing beginners. Therefore, understanding and experimenting with ratios is critical to customizing your juices.

THE 80/20 RULE: VEGETABLE DOMINANT JUICING

As a beginner venturing into the world of juicing, it's crucial to grasp a basic rule of thumb to ensure your juices are palatable and nutritionally balanced. This fundamental guideline is the 80/20 rule, suggesting that your juice concoctions should ideally comprise approximately 80% vegetables and 20% fruits.

WHY IS THIS RATIO SO CRUCIAL?

Balancing Sugar Content

The first factor to consider is sugar content. Although fruits are brimming with essential vitamins and antioxidants, they are also high in natural sugars. When consumed in juice, the body absorbs these sugars much more quickly because the fiber, which would ordinarily slow this process, has been removed. This rapid absorption can lead to significant spikes in your blood sugar levels.

On the other hand, vegetables generally contain less sugar than fruits. Therefore, by adhering to the 80/20 rule, you can create a nutrient-rich juice while keeping the sugar content relatively low.

Optimizing Nutrient Intake

Vegetables are superstars when it comes to nutrient density. They are packed with various vitamins, minerals, and beneficial compounds. By having a higher proportion of vegetables, your juice will contain a broader range of these vital nutrients. The remaining 20% fruit content serves a crucial function too. Adding fruit can enhance the overall flavor of the juice, making it more pleasant to drink. This is especially useful for beginners who might still need to become accustomed to the more pungent tastes of certain vegetables.

Here's a practical example using the 80/20 rule:
Balanced Green Juice

- 160g of cucumbers (25 calories)
- 120g of spinach (28 calories)
- 40g of green apples (21 calories)
- 30g of lemon (8 calories)

Kara Kemp

In this recipe, cucumbers and spinach comprise 80% of the total weight, providing a rich source of vitamins and minerals. The apple and lemon constitute the remaining 20%, adding a touch of sweetness and a bit of zing to enhance the flavor of the juice.

Remember, the 80/20 rule is a guideline, not an absolute law. Feel free to adjust the ratios to your liking as you become more experienced in juicing. After all, the best juice is the one you enjoy drinking and serves your nutritional needs best. Enjoy the journey!

BALANCING TASTE AND NUTRITION

The beauty of juicing lies in its duality: it can offer both a burst of tantalizing flavors and a power-packed punch of vital nutrients. However, striking the right balance between taste and nutrition can be an art. This section aims to guide you in creating juices that satisfy your palate while providing your body with the necessary nourishment.

Understanding Your Ingredients

Every fruit and vegetable comes with its unique nutrient profile and flavor. Some vegetables like kale and spinach are nutrient powerhouses, but their intense flavors might be challenging for beginners. On the other hand, fruits like apples and pineapples are sweet and flavorful, but they also have higher sugar content.

Understanding your ingredients' nutritional and flavor profiles is the first step toward creating balanced juices. This understanding allows you to mix and match components to optimize taste and nutrition.

The Sweetness Factor

Fruits are often used to sweeten vegetable-heavy juices, making them more enjoyable, especially for beginners. While this is a great way to make your juices tastier, remember that fruits also have a significant sugar load. Therefore, it's vital to use fruits judiciously.

A good rule of thumb is to limit fruits to around 20% of your juice, as suggested in the previous section (The 80/20 Rule: Vegetable Dominant Juicing). However, adjust this based on your dietary needs and taste preferences.

Adding a 'Zing'

Citrus fruits like lemons and limes or spicy elements like ginger can add a 'zing' to your juice, making it more vibrant and exciting. These ingredients also come with health benefits. For example, ginger is known for its anti-inflammatory properties, while lemons are packed with vitamin C.

Don't Forget the Greens

Green leafy vegetables are among the most nutrient-dense foods out there. They are packed with vitamins, minerals, and antioxidants. Incorporating a variety of greens into your juices ensures you're getting a wide range of nutrients. If you're new to green juices, start with milder greens like spinach or lettuce and gradually work your way up to stronger-tasting ones like kale or arugula.

Playing with Ratios

The key to balancing taste and nutrition lies in playing with ratios. Once you understand your ingredients, you can adjust their proportions to create delicious, nutrient-dense juices. Keep experimenting until you find combinations that you enjoy and that align with your nutritional goals.

Balancing taste and nutrition in juicing might require trial and error, but it's rewarding. As you get more comfortable, you can create a wide array of delightful and healthful juices tailored to your preferences. Happy juicing!

Kara Kemp

UNDERSTANDING FLAVOR PROFILES

To effectively create your juice recipes, it's essential to understand the flavor profiles of the fruits and vegetables you'll be using. Just like a chef needs to know how different ingredients interact to create a delicious meal, a juice-maker should understand how the tastes of diverse produce blend together to make a satisfying juice. This section will guide you through the primary flavor profiles and how to combine them effectively.

Sweet

Sweet fruits are often the backbone of a good juice, providing an appealing taste that can balance out less palatable ingredients. Apples, pineapples, and oranges are fruits that naturally sweetness your juice. However,

Tart

Tart or sour ingredients can add a refreshing kick to your juices. They help cut through the sweetness of fruit and can brighten the flavor profile. Lemons, limes, and certain berries like blackberries and raspberries can provide this tartness.

Earthy

Many vegetables have an earthy flavor profile. Beetroot, carrots, and spinach are all examples. These ingredients provide a grounding base for your juice. They can also contribute essential nutrients, including beta-carotene, iron, and other vitamins and minerals.

Bitter

Bitterness can add complexity to your juice but should be used sparingly, especially if you're a beginner. Too much anger can make a juice unpalatable. Greens like kale and arugula are often associated with a bitter flavor profile.

Juicing for beginners

Spicy

Ingredients like ginger, turmeric, and even small hot peppers can add a spicy kick to your juices. This spiciness can make fluid more exciting and also provides additional health benefits. Both ginger and turmeric, for example, are known for their anti-inflammatory properties.

Balancing Flavors

Understanding these flavor profiles is the first step in creating a balanced juice. Generally, a well-balanced juice will have a combination of these flavors. For instance, an apple (sweet), lemon (tart), spinach (earthy), a small piece of ginger (spicy), and a hint of kale (bitter) can make for a balanced and nutritious green juice.

Remember, taste is highly subjective. What one person finds delicious, another might not. The goal is to find the balance that works for you. Start by following recipes, then as you become more comfortable, feel free to experiment with these flavors. Keep tasting and adjusting until you find your perfect blend.

Understanding flavor profiles and how they blend is an essential part of the journey toward becoming a skilled juice maker. So don't be afraid to experiment and discover your favorite combinations. Happy juicing!

Kara Kemp

Part 6: Juicing and Meal Planning

Juicing is an excellent way to ensure you get various nutrients from fruits and vegetables, but it shouldn't replace your regular meals. Instead, think of it as a supplement to a balanced diet. Here's how you can effectively incorporate juicing into your meal planning:

1. Start Your Day Right

One of the best times to have juice is on an empty stomach first thing in the morning. This allows the nutrients in the liquid to be quickly absorbed by your body. Fresh juice in the morning helps to hydrate your body, wakes up your digestive system, and provides a quick energy boost.

2. A Mid-Morning or Afternoon Snack

Consider having fresh juice instead of reaching for a coffee or a sugary snack during that mid-morning or afternoon slump. It'll provide you with a natural energy boost and help curb any cravings and keep you feeling full until your next meal.

3. Before or After a Workout

Fresh juices are also a tremendous pre-or post-workout snack. A fruit-based juice before your workout can provide a quick source of energy. After your workout, a juice from fruits and vegetables can help replenish electrolytes, rehydrate your body, and aid recovery

4. Meal Replacement (Occasionally)

While replacing meals with juice regularly is not advisable, doing so occasionally can give your digestive system a break. If you choose to replace a meal with juice, make sure it's nutrient-dense - include a good mix of fruits, vegetables, and perhaps some protein like chia seeds or Greek yogurt.

5. Planning Your Juices

As part of your meal planning, decide on which days and when you want to include juices. Depending on your schedule, you should make your juices fresh each time or prepare a few days' worth in advance.

When meal planning, be mindful of the sugar content in your juices - remember that vegetables should form the bulk of your juices, with fruit used sparingly for sweetness. Try to include a wide variety of fruits and vegetables in your juices over the week to ensure you get a range of nutrients.

By incorporating juicing into your meal planning, you can ensure that you're getting the maximum benefits from this nutritious practice without negatively impacting your overall diet. Remember, balance and variety are essential to a healthy diet, and while juicing can be a part of this, it should complement a diet rich in whole, unprocessed foods.

Kara Kemp

A 30-DAY JUICING PROGRAM WITH MEAL PLAN

In this chapter, we offer you a step-by-step guide to integrating juicing into your everyday life. This 30-day journey includes a juice recipe for each day and a balanced meal plan. Remember, the goal of this program is to amplify the intake of nutrients, not to replace whole foods with juices. Each body is different, so please consult your healthcare provider or nutritionist before starting this or any meal plan.

Daily Routine:

Upon Rising: Warm water with lemon juice.
Breakfast: A nutritious option like oatmeal topped with fruits and nuts, whole grain toast with avocado, or a Greek yogurt parfait.
Mid-Morning Snack: A handful of mixed nuts or seeds.
Lunch: A large salad or a bowl of hearty soup, coupled with your freshly prepared juice.
Afternoon Snack: A piece of fruit like an apple or a pear.
Dinner: A well-rounded meal consisting of lean protein, complex carbs, and various vegetables.
Before Bed: Use herbal tea of your choice, such as chamomile or peppermint.

Juicing for beginners

Day-by-Day Juice Recipes and Meal Suggestions:

Day 1
Juice Recipe: 2 green apples, one cucumber, 1 cup spinach, 1/2 lemon

Dinner: Grilled chicken with quinoa and roasted Brussels sprouts.

Day 2
Juice Recipe: 1/2 pineapple, 1 mango, 1/2 lime

Dinner: Baked salmon, sweet potato mash, and sauteed kale.

Day 3
Juice Recipe: 2 oranges, one grapefruit, 1/2 lemon

Dinner: Lentil soup with a side of multigrain bread.

Day 4
Juice Recipe: 1 beetroot, one carrot, two oranges

Dinner: Turkey meatballs with spaghetti squash and marinara sauce.

Day 5
Juice Recipe: 1 cucumber, two kiwis, one green apple

Dinner: Tofu stir-fry with brown rice and assorted veggies.

Day 6
Juice Recipe: 2 oranges, one grapefruit, one small piece of ginger

Dinner: Vegetable stir-fry with tofu and brown rice.

Day 7
Juice Recipe: 2 cups of spinach, one cucumber, two green apples

Dinner: Lentil and vegetable curry served with whole-grain naan.

Day 8
Juice Recipe: 1 cup of pineapple, one mango, one kiwi

Dinner: Baked cod with roasted sweet potatoes and sautéed spinach.

Day 9
Juice Recipe: 1 beetroot, one carrot, one apple, 1/2 lemon

Dinner: Grilled chicken salad with mixed greens, cherry tomatoes, cucumbers, and a vinaigrette **dressing.**

Day 10
Juice Recipe: 2 grapefruits, one lemon, one lime

Dinner: Quinoa salad with chickpeas, cherry tomatoes, Cucumber, and a lemon-tahini dressing.

.

118

Kara Kemp

Day 11

Juice Recipe: 2 cups of mixed berries, one apple, 1/2 lemon

Dinner: Baked salmon with a side of steamed broccoli and brown rice.

Day 12

Juice Recipe: 2 green apples, 1/2 lemon, 1-inch piece of ginger

Dinner: Vegetable stir-fry with lean chicken or tofu and quinoa.

Day 13

Juice Recipe: 1 cup of red cabbage, one beet, one carrot, one apple

Dinner: Baked trout with a side of sautéed spinach and sweet potatoes.

Day 14

Juice Recipe: 1 cup pineapple, one orange, 1/2 grapefruit

Dinner: Stuffed bell peppers with ground turkey, tomatoes, and mixed greens.

Day 15

Juice Recipe: 2 cups of spinach, one cucumber, two stalks of celery, one apple

Dinner: Grilled shrimp skewers with a quinoa salad.

Day 16

Juice Recipe: 2 apples, one pear, 1/2 a lemon

Dinner: Whole grain pasta with marinara sauce, mixed vegetables, and roasted Brussels

sprouts.

Day 17

Juice Recipe: 1 cup of mixed berries, 1/2 a lemon, one apple

Dinner: Grilled salmon with a side of roasted asparagus and couscous.

Day 18

Juice Recipe: 2 oranges, one grapefruit, 1/2 lemon

Dinner: Grilled chicken salad with cherry tomatoes, avocado, and a vinaigrette dressing.

Day 19

Juice Recipe: 2 cups of kale, two green apples, one cucumber

Dinner: Baked tilapia with a side of quinoa and sautéed spinach.

Day 20

Juice Recipe: 2 beets, one carrot, one apple, 1/2 lemon

Dinner: Vegetable curry with brown rice.

Day 21

Juice Recipe: 1 cup pineapple, one mango, one banana

Dinner: Lentil soup with a side of whole-grain bread.

Juicing for beginners

Day 22

Juice Recipe: 2 cups spinach, one cucumber, two stalks of celery, one green apple

Dinner: Grilled turkey burger with sweet potato fries and mixed greens.

Day 23

Juice Recipe: 1 cup mixed berries, one apple, 1/2 lemon

Dinner: Baked cod with a side of roasted vegetables and couscous.

Day 24

Juice Recipe: 1 orange, two carrots, one apple, 1/2-inch piece of ginger

Dinner: Tofu stir-fry with colorful vegetables served over brown rice.

Day 25

Juice Recipe: 2 cups of spinach, one cucumber, two stalks of celery, one pear

Dinner: Baked chicken with a side of roasted Brussels sprouts and quinoa.

Day 26

Juice Recipe: 1 cup pineapple, one banana, 1/2 cup of coconut water

Dinner: Vegetable-stuffed bell peppers with a side of sweet potato mash.

Day 27

Juice Recipe: 1 beet, one apple, one carrot, 1/2 lemon

Dinner: Baked salmon with a side of sautéed asparagus and wild rice.

Day 28

Juice Recipe: 1 green apple, one cucumber, two stalks of celery, 1/2 lemon

Dinner: Grilled shrimp with a side of mixed greens and quinoa salad.

Day 29

Juice Recipe: 1 cup mixed berries, one apple, 1/2 banana

Dinner: Lean turkey meatballs with whole grain pasta and marinara sauce.

Day 30

Juice Recipe: 1 cup of kale, one green apple, one cucumber, 1/2 lemon, 1-inch piece of ginger

Dinner: Baked cod with sautéed spinach and sweet potato fries.

Congratulations! You've completed the 30-day juicing journey. We hope these juice recipes and meal suggestions have helped you to incorporate more fruits and vegetables into your diet and experience the benefits of a healthier lifestyle. Remember to always listen to your body and adjust your diet accordingly. Consistency is the key to long-term health, so keep up the excellent work and make juicing a part of your daily routine!

Conclusion

As we've journeyed through the world of juicing, I have aimed to demystify this practice and present it in a manner that makes it accessible, enjoyable, and beneficial for all. From understanding the basics of juicing to exploring the vast array of fruits and vegetables you can juice to finally venturing into creating our own healthful, nutrient-packed juice concoctions, I hope you've found this book enlightening and inspiring.

What's more, we've delved into the practical aspects of juicing and the underlying nutritional science that makes juicing such a potentially healthful practice. We've seen how juicing can support everything from digestion to detoxification, immunity to energy levels, and even weight loss.

Moreover, this book has sought to underline the importance of balance and variety in your juicing journey. The shared recipes range from simple, single-ingredient juices to more complex blends incorporating various fruits, vegetables, and even spices. This spectrum of recipes aims to encourage you to experiment with different combinations and discover what suits your palate and nutritional needs best.

As we conclude, remember that juicing is a tool to enhance a balanced, healthful diet, not a magic bullet or a standalone solution. Always aim to maintain a diverse diet, with juicing as an additional nutrient-dense, easily digestible nourishment source. Above all, listen to your body and adjust your juicing practices to fit your unique health and wellness needs.

Finally, remember to enjoy the process. Whether trying out a new juice recipe or experimenting with unexpected ingredient combinations, please keep an open mind and have fun with it. After all, the joy of creating something delicious and healthful from scratch is part of the charm of juicing.

Thank you for coming along on this journey with me. Here's to your health and to many refreshing, nourishing, and delicious juices in your future. Happy juicing!

Appendix

Kara Kemp

Appendix

Appendix

Kara Kemp

Appendix

Made in the USA
Las Vegas, NV
17 October 2023

79133842R00072